MASTERPIECES

OF EUROPEAN PAINTING
IN AMERICA

MASTERPIECES
OF EUROPEAN PAINTING
IN AMERICA

WITH 317 REPRODUCTIONS

EDITED BY PROFESSOR HANS TIETZE

OXFORD UNIVERSITY PRESS · NEW YORK

FOREWORD

A general history of art-collecting in the United States of North America, which no one has hitherto attempted to write, would throw an interesting light on the economic and cultural development of the country; all the tendencies of one hundred and fifty years of independent national existence have left their mark in the activities of collectors, in those objects which for some particular reason were brought together and preserved, and in those which were denied this privilege.

The scope of the present volume is far less ambitious. It deals with only a part of the vast artistic material which for one reason or another has been collected—with the works of European painting down to the end of the nineteenth century. If on the one hand this limitation to Europe—that is to say, a civilization foreign to America but deriving from a common ancestry—and the exclusion of contemporary works denotes a narrowing of the field, on the other hand it throws into better relief the essential problem of art-collecting; remoteness of space and time emphasizes the peculiarity of art, the value which we put upon art being always in conscious opposition to normal life. This quality of contrast is in part due to the ethical nature of art itself: art is the unusual element which from the earliest times has stood apart from the world of everyday life; obviously it is all the more so when the place and time of its creation differ completely from the too familiar now and here. One result of this element in the nature of art is that the first contact with it always begets "an unintelligent curiosity about something which is unusual and wonderful"; in Europe this conception produced the "Chambers of Curiosities" of the sixteenth century; in America it was fought as late as the second half of the nineteenth century by James J. Jarves, the prophet of a new way of thinking, whose words we have just quoted above to characterize this tendency.

His indictment is not altogether unjustified. The first American museum—founded, it should be noted, by so original an artist as Charles Wilson Peale—at Philadelphia, started in 1785 with the skeleton of a mastodon which had just been unearthed, and later assembled in one room Peale's portraits of celebrated Americans and a collection of stuffed birds. The museum founded in 1790 at Manhattan by the Tammany Society, the objects of which were supposed to be American history and natural history, announced that "any object, from whatever country it might come," was welcome, and found its logical conclusion in Barnum's show, which also absorbed other successors of that first museum—for example, Reuben Peale's Museum and Gallery of the Fine Arts. In the Far West, where many survivals of the early period still put up a tough resistance, Sutro's Baths in San Francisco, with their curious medley of natural objects and the products of civilization, preserve even to this day the memory of such primitive collections of curiosities. But even on a higher plane it was curiosity which for a long time preceded real interest in art. In 1828 Louis David's "Coronation of Napoleon" and later Munkaczy's and Millet's great productions were taken round the country in a sensational manner, and even the first introductions to the public of Bryan's art collection, of the "Düsseldorf Gallery" and J. J. Jarves's fine collection were accompanied by all the tricks of publicity, with a view to awakening the interest of the public.

That the hard soil of the New World offered more stubborn resistance to the penetration of art than the more richly nurtured soil of the Old World may be easily explained as due to the backwardness of the newly liberated colony and of its economic development, and also to the Puritan ideas of its inhabitants. Both these circumstances were unfavourable to the furthering of art. Harding's grandfather, who wrote to his grandson after the latter had become a painter: "Settle down on your farm and lead the life of an honest man," was certainly a man of humble origin; but even to the literary leaders of the nation everything connected with aesthetics was suspect until after the middle of the century. "Where beauty is sought after not in the sense of religion and love, but for the purpose of pleasure, it degrades the seeker," was the doctrine of Emerson, and even Hawthorne—despite the many years he spent in Italy and his earnest attempts to understand art—could never quite overcome his puritanical mistrust of it. "A deep understanding for painting and sculpture, and perhaps also for music, seems to have been peculiar to men who were capable of every crime against human society and seems to have formed a fine and hard varnish over their characters," he writes in his Roman diary. Art was suspect even to those whom their talent impelled to paint. The Quaker painter, Edward Hicks, author of the popular pictures of William Penn's treaty with the Indians, of the Declaration of Independence, and of the "Reign of Peace upon Earth," wrote in his diary in 1843: " Painting seems to me to be one of those arts which say nothing and signify nothing, which have never brought any real profit to mankind. But as the inseparable companion of lust and pride, it has foretold the fall of empires and kingdoms; and in my opinion it is now one of the warning signs of the rapid decline of the American Republic."

Two influences helped to overcome this intellectual viewpoint, which was undoubtedly shared by the majority of the American people: acquaintance with foreign art and the penetration of Ruskin's ethically coloured artistic doctrines.

A few old works of art are mentioned in certain private collections of the eighteenth century—John Watson at Perth Amboy about 1725, Smibert 1728, Hamilton, Robert Gilmor—but it is impossible to obtain an idea of their importance; somewhat richer was the material which the backwash of the French Revolution and the Napoleonic wars carried across the Atlantic. In John Trumbull's collection, which was exhibited at the Park Theatre, New York, in 1804–5, and in Joseph Bonaparte's collection at Borden-town, New Jersey, which Sully visited and described in 1826, there were pictures by old masters, and especially by those who were popular with collectors in Europe—the lesser Dutch masters, Van Dyck, Poussin, etc. In the Gallery of Fine Arts which the merchant Luman Reed installed in 1844 in his house at 13 Greenwich Street, and opened to the public, there were—in addition to works by American artists—pictures by Fyt, Morland, and Annibale Carracci; the catalogue exalts the value of such a collection in high-sounding words, which are clearly meant to be a defence of art against the moral obloquy which was its lot in the country: A picture-gallery in a town is a source of refinement; nay, even more, a stronghold of virtue; representations of heroism and patriotism elevate our minds above everyday commonplaces to noble and pious sentiments.

The same assertion of the moral value of art is emphasized in the catalogues of two other collections, which were important for the development of art-collecting in America in the middle of the nineteenth century because they were the first to present foreign art on a large scale: these were the "Düsseldorf Gallery" which John G. Boker formed in 1849 out of the works of contemporary painters of the Düsseldorf school—Hasenclever, Schrödter, Camphausen, Andreas and Oswald Achenbach, Leutze, Steinbruck—and about thirty Italian pictures which Thomas J. Bryan brought to America in 1853 and which subsequently came into the hands of the Historical Society in New York. The catalogue of the former dates from 1851, that of the Bryan collection from 1853—the latter bears the characteristic title: "Companion to the Bryan Gallery of Christian Art." Both these catalogues attach the greatest importance to the associations called forth by the subjects of the pictures; these two collections, though their lives were short and their quality negligible, must at least be accorded the merit of having drawn attention to the essence of artistic beauty and historical development, but their promoters had not the courage to base their opinions on the value of works of art on a purely artistic foundation.

This was done by James Jackson Jarves, for whom art was the most important element in life. The descendant of a Huguenot family which had emigrated from England to America, from 1848 on he spent several years in France and Italy, collecting works of art and participating in the struggle waged by the European Romantics and Pre-Raphaelites for the recognition of primitive, naïve, "genuine" art. This tendency coincided with that transformation of taste, of which the most striking manifestation was the reorganization of the National Gallery in London in the year 1853. As examples of his artistic doctrines, influenced by Ruskin, Jarves brought back with him a choice collection of 145 Italian primitives, which were exhibited in 1860–1 at the Institute of Fine Arts, New York, and in 1863 at the home of the Historical Society. Despite Jarves's efforts, however, and the support of the Harvard teacher of art, Charles Eliot Norton, it was impossible to find a permanent home for these pictures, until in 1868 they were deposited at Yale University as security for a loan of twenty thousand dollars. When they were subsequently auctioned, because Jarves was unable to repay the loan, no bidders could be found, so that Yale University, almost against its will, became the owner of a collection which is now regarded as a treasure-house of early Italian art.

The hostility caused by Jarves's efforts on behalf of art was directed not only against his belief in the oneness of art and life—which to the puritanically minded was bound to appear an exaggeration of the value of art—but also against the vigour with which he proclaimed the supreme virtues of early art. Just as Constable thirty years before (1822) had opposed the project of creating a National Gallery of old masters in London on the grounds that it would mean the end of independent national art in England, so in America (in the *Crayon*, August 1855) similar attacks were made on Jarves's collection: "We need no disciples of art, we only need men who with bared heads and open hearts and eyes will stand in the presence of Nature . . . we do not believe that all the pictures in Europe could make any artist greater even by the breadth of a finger." The Jarves collection was a symptom of that subordination to European art to which America had to submit; but also—despite the lack of understanding of its exceptional value—it was a challenge to Americans to pay more attention to great art.

Jarves was one of the pioneers in the struggle to obtain a public art museum for New York, an idea which gradually matured. The art exhibition held in 1864 in aid of the sick and wounded of the national army—The Metropolitan Fair Picture Gallery—comprised many modern European pictures from private collections; among the many thousand visitors to this exhibition the desire began to spread to have a permanent art gallery. Three years later, in his *Book of the Artists*, Henry T. Tuckermann—referring expressly to the enthusiasm aroused by the exhibition—described the project of creating a gallery accessible to all as being just as much a duty for a great city like New York as the maintenance of public hospitals and libraries. The realization of this project was already taking shape—it was suggested for the first time at the Fourth of July dinner in 1866 of the American Society in Paris; the various phases of the campaign have been described in detail by Winfred E. Howe in his history of the Metropolitan Museum (New York, 1913). Here we will only mention the most important event in the early period of the museum, its transfer in 1880 to its third and permanent home. When the museum was opened, it was able to show not only the fruits of the campaign for the purchase of pictures which had been carried on energetically since 1869—the opportunities offered by the Franco-Prussian War in 1870–1 having been exploited to the full—but also 250 pictures on loan from private collections, of which three-eighths were American and five-eighths of European origin. William K. Vanderbilt had cabled from Europe that ten of his own pictures might be selected for this purpose.

With the founding of the Metropolitan Museum in New York, America assumed its place in the international sphere of art-collecting. It was not the first institution in America to exhibit European as well as American works of art; there existed at an earlier date the collection of the Wadsworth Atheneum, Hartford, the museum at Boston, of which the 1847 catalogue includes various European artists, and at Yale the Jarves collection which the University had acquired almost against its will. The novelty in connection with the Metropolitan Museum was that it was to become a steadily growing collection of international art, working in collaboration with private collectors and thus providing the latter with a purpose and a definite trend. As early as the 1860's the number of private collections was increasing rapidly—the above-mentioned book by Tuckermann mentions quite a number in various parts of the United States—but it was only when the Metropolitan Museum was opened that their local and purely American character yielded to an increasing interest in European art. The international exhibition held at Philadelphia in 1876 to celebrate the centenary of the United States was a triumph for contemporary French art and for the English masters of the early nineteenth century. When the Metropolitan Museum was opened in 1880, the private collections in New York already constituted a valuable source of material.

During the next fifty years there took place that tremendous transplantation of art treasures which, in the series of wireless talks on art in America given in 1934 (*Art in America*, 1934, p. 43), was compared to the great removals of works of art in the past —the plundering of Greece by the Romans or Napoleon's forcible removal of European art objects to Paris. The scattered, inconsiderable examples of ancient art were replaced by a fantastic treasure-house, in which every school of European painting was represented. In this rush to collect works of art, itself a symptom of the increasing vitality of American life during those decades, private and public collections show phases which differ only in point of time; the private collections were the organs of the public galleries; the former always kept the latter in mind. Except for a few cases which may be disregarded, the private collections—in accordance with the American conception of the duties of wealth —have come under public control, even though they may not actually be public property. The large numbers of European masterpieces which are the boast of American museums, were acquired mainly as a result of the initiative and energy of private collectors, who, however, did not, like the pioneers of an earlier generation, Thomas J. Bryan and James Jackson Jarves, devote their whole lives and energies to art, but merely employed the spare time left over from their other activities in forming art-collections. Those who now became the leading collectors, such as William K. Vanderbilt and Catherine Lorillard Wolfe, were of an entirely new type. The sudden rise in the quantity and quality of collections and the rapid increase of market prices for works of art made such great wealth a necessary premise of art-collecting that only a successful business career could provide it with the necessary foundation. In consequence the aim of collecting also changed. For Bryan and Jarves devotion to art had been a reason for living, but for the new collectors art was merely an ornament, the fulfilment of an ambition or the satisfaction of pride, or an addition to the profits drawn from a more than average display of energy. Different people achieved different results with their collections. Some were seized by the mania for quantity and systematically endeavoured to attain completeness in one sphere or the greatest possible degree of variety; at Philadelphia, John G. Johnson tried to have a specimen of every artist mentioned in the history of art in his collection; and at Baltimore Henry Walters accumulated such a mass of art objects that after the transformation of his great house into a museum four-fifths of them had to be kept shut up in repositories. Others aimed at assembling an harmonious collection of all kinds of treasures which should form a princely framework to their existence—like Benjamin Altman in New York and Joseph Widener in his country house at Elkins Park—or were satisfied with ennobling their bourgeois surroundings by means of arts and crafts— Charles P. Taft in Cincinnati and Philip Lehmann in New York. Others again showed themselves able—like Mr. and Mrs. H. O. Havemeyer in New York—thanks to their boldness and the sureness of their artistic judgment, to open up new paths for collectors. Sometimes all these varied impulses—the desire for acquisition for its own sake, the taste for decorative effects, and the pleasures of artistic discovery—united to form a passionate joy in art, which in the case of Mrs. Isabella Stewart Gardner of Boston became the essential element in her life, while in the case of Pierpont Morgan it took the form of a grandiose organization, similar to that of his business enterprises.

This enumeration, limited to the most prominent among them, of so many different types of collectors reminds us that the collection of works of art in America is not—as European pride would sometimes lead us to believe—the automatic consequence of a superiority of financial means, but, like every other cultural movement, has been determined by certain creative individuals. Though mere money and the desire for social advancement may have contributed something, it is nevertheless true that other qualities characteristic of the peculiarly American form of art-collecting may be discerned in these prominent members of the collecting classes: ruthless energy, so closely bound up with the qualities which are successfully developed in the course of the economic struggle; the determination to catch up with older civilized countries who in this field have had so long a start; the desire, derived from the American attitude towards public service, to make the collected works of art an instrument of cultural education; and lastly the freedom from deep-rooted prejudices which made it possible for America to render pioneer service to impartial art-collecting. Whereas J. J. Jarves had only to struggle against the indifference of his unprepared fellow-countrymen, efforts made at the same time and in the same direction in Europe encountered the obstinate resistance of an older generation, for whom the works of the Primitives—in the words of one of the conservative Trustees of the National Gallery—were not art, but merely antiquities. Right from the beginning American collectors were less prejudiced and more progressive than those of Europe. Norton acquired his beautiful collection of the works of Blake and bequeathed it to the Boston Museum, before the fellow-countrymen of that mystic had discovered that he was one of the greatest English artists; John G. Johnson and William van Horne purchased pictures by Cézanne at a time when no collector of their rank in Europe would have dreamt of making such an experiment. It is to this daring on the part of a few pioneers that American collections owe their superiority in certain fields of collecting which were untrodden until the second half of the nineteenth century. If America is so astonishingly rich in the works of Rembrandt, Vermeer, and El Greco, the explanation is not merely that American collectors were rich enough to outbid all competitors, but also that they had the courage to step in at the right time; Martin A. Ryerson's instinctive interest for primitive art and J. P. Morgan's for early medieval art were the beginnings of a development which has been carried on by Alexander J. Cassats, Mrs. Potter Palmer, and J. H. Whittemore at Naugatuck (Conn.) as regards French Impressionist painting, and by the Lewisohns, Chester Dales, and Dr. Barnes at Merion for the Post-Impressionists. Collectors of this kind have won for America, which came too late to obtain more than a second choice of the works of classical art, the foremost position in other fields.

In all this it is impossible to draw any distinction between public and private collections, because, as we have mentioned above, they were two phases of the same activity. Of the private collections already named, most—and many others we have not mentioned —have now become public property, partly through transformation, partly because they have been absorbed in museums. Of the oldest collections those of Bryan and Dürr were the basis of the museum of the Historical Society in New York, that of Jarves became the art collection of Yale University, New Haven, while the Corcoran collection became the museum of that name in Washington. In addition to this the Marquard, Altman, Havemeyer, and Friedsam collections have passed, with others, to the Metropolitan Museum, New York; the Holden collection, which also derives from Jarves's, to the Cleveland Museum; the Libbey collection to the Toledo Museum; the Emery collection to the musem in Cincinnati; the Clark collection to the Corcoran Gallery in Washington; the van der Lip collection to the museum in Minneapolis, the Ryerson and Coeburn collections to the Art Institute, Chicago. Other collections have become independent museums, for example the Isabella Stewart Gardner collection in Boston, the John G. Johnson collection in Philadelphia, the Taft collection in Cincinnati, the H. Walters collection in Baltimore, the T. B. Walker collection in Minneapolis, and the J. B. Croker collection at Sacramento; others, while still remaining private property, are now, owing to the liberality with which admission is granted, to all intents and purposes public institutions, for example the Widener collection at Elkins Park, the Huntington collection at San Marino, California, the Pierpont Morgan Library in New York. Others, too, have followed this example, such as the Henry C. Frick Museum in New York, which has been a public museum since the autumn of 1935, and the G. L. Winthrop collection, New York, which, after the death of its owner, is to be handed over to the Fogg Art Museum, Cambridge, Mass. The magnificent Andrew W. Mellon collection, which will probably form the proud conclusion to the history of American art-collecting, is to form a National Gallery in the capital of the Union. And it is hoped that many other still existing private collections will ultimately undergo a similar transformation.

From the above list, which comprises only the most important and moreover is limited to collections of European paintings, it is evident that the independent acquisitions of museums are at present only of secondary importance in comparison with this main source of paintings. The public galleries are for the most part not the outcome of a systematic scheme of collecting, but, considered separately, an agglomeration of several private collections, and considered together, the permanent result of the activity of collectors throughout the country. That has its advantages and disadvantages. They are far more closely connected with the public consciousness of art than is usually the case with European galleries, and for this reason they have a more pedagogic tendency; they are conscious that they play a part in the education of the country, art being interpreted by them as a living force which continues to exert its influence through their present activity. From the present we may deduce the past. The way in which the Barnes Foundation at Merion and the Philipps Memorial Gallery in Washington, both through their composition and arrangement and through the literary attainments and the gift for lecturing of their founders and supporters, endeavour to emphasize the importance of art in the spiritual life of the individual and of the nation, is not only a renewal of the oldest tradition in American art-collecting, but also coincides with the ideas of American individualism, which imposes upon the individual the duty of serving the common weal.

It is easy to see what are the disadvantages of this individualism. The works which became public property had not undergone any process of sifting, and sometimes were not altogether irreproachable. Not only was all systematic activity on the part of the museums hampered, but in some cases the donations were accompanied by precise and onerous conditions. Works which were obviously of inferior quality could not always be excluded, and in some cases not even an alteration of the attribution was allowed. Side by side with much that was of the very first quality the museums received much that was of little account, and in fact it was in this way that—as we said above—they became the permanent result of the activity of collectors throughout the country. American collectors —like those of all other countries—did not always combine technical competence with the possession of material means; through lack of training and, until a short time ago, through lack of first-rate comparative material, the American collector was more liable than those of other countries to be attracted by the fashions of the moment and to rely on the advice of experts and dealers. Such advice, especially in the first years of a collecting career, was not always reliable or disinterested. There is all the more reason for admitting now that the credulity of inexperienced collectors has been abused, because, with the energy characteristic of American methods, the defects have now been made good. Better training, the increasing number of good paintings and of first-class experts to be found in America itself, have raised the average standard of collecting in general, though it is true that these advantages benefit mainly the Eastern States, where a tradition of collecting has already existed for several generations. If one journeys from the Atlantic to the Pacific seaboard, one traverses, so to speak, the early history of American collecting. In the West there are still public and private collections which answer the descriptions of those which existed fifty or sixty years ago in the East; doubtless the difference will be eliminated in a relatively short time and copies and forgeries will be excluded from the collections of the newer States as well, quantity will be replaced by quality, and mere accumulation by systematic selection. This is a process which coincides with the rapid growth and maturing of America in general; the transition from extensive to intensive economy will run its course in the field of art as well.

The material which America acquired in the first of these two phases is astonishingly large, although uneven in composition and quality. All European schools of all times are represented to such an extent that the advantages and disadvantages which accompanied the assembling of the material become clearly visible. Of the two schools which were the first to awaken interest, the Italian is more strongly represented by early works, the Netherlandish school by its late period; in the former case this is due to the example of Jarves and also to the influence of Ruskin and the Pre-Raphaelites which Norton transmitted to Harvard; in the case of the Netherlandish school it is due to the fact that the wave of Impressionism brought with it a full understanding of the later Rembrandt and Frans Hals and also of Jan Vermeer. In addition to this two great advisers of American collectors, B. Berenson and Wilhelm von Bode, have exercised a salutary influence. Only in comparatively recent times have the Dutch Primitives and Italian Baroque become better represented, while the classical middle period, the Italian High Renaissance and the sixteenth-century painters of the Netherlands are still inadequately represented, because the chief works from this period formed the basis of European collections and for this reason seldom come into the market.

When we turn to the representation in American collections of the Spanish and British schools, we find a reflection of world economic conditions. The impoverishment of Spain in the second half of the nineteenth century and the grave losses suffered by wealthy British families in the War have unlocked the doors of many collections which hitherto had been jealously guarded. America was spiritually ready and materially able to take advantage of this. It has received important works of Spanish art from all periods, and has created a special centre for them in the collections of the Hispanic Society of New York; of the painters of the "golden century," Murillo, whose works were mostly in the hands of the Church in Spain, is only sporadically represented; of the painter to the Royal Family, Velazquez, we find for the most part only early works which had hitherto been passed over; while El Greco, whose fame spread outside Spain only with the Post-Impressionist movement, is better represented in America than anywhere outside his adopted country. Of British artists, the great landscape-painters of the early nineteenth century have been popular since the 1870's; the doors of the great ancestral collections were not opened until the post-war crisis, which has brought to the Huntington collection in San Marino, California, the choicest gems of British portraiture. No American purchase was such a blow to British pride as the acquisition in 1922 by Henry E. Huntington of Gainsborough's "Blue Boy."

The older schools of France and Germany make a less imposing show. In both of these countries a long-established interest in art has kept a jealous eye on the national artistic heritage, so that only unwanted pictures reached foreign collections, and even these, as far as French art is concerned, were preserved in many cases in Germany and Russia, and as regards German art, in England. By these circuitous routes America has come into possession of a number of works, notably of several portraits by Holbein, who, as painter to the English Court, has had to share the subsequent fate of the rest of British social painting. On the whole, however, the great French and German masters—Poussin and Watteau, Dürer and Grünewald—are the most inadequately represented in America.

France, however, takes its revenge with the painting of the nineteenth century, which supplanted all other European schools in the interest of collectors. Originally German artists of this period were the most prized, and we have heard how the "Düsseldorf Gallery" was one of the kindergartens of art collecting in America. But the works of the Munich and Düsseldorf painters, which at first predominated in the East and Middle

West, were either too bad or too badly chosen to hold their ground for long. Even in museums like those of Cincinnati, St. Louis, and Milwaukee—like the works of French "Salon" painting which followed immediately after them—they have for the most part been relegated to the repositories; only in the E. B. Croker Museum at Sacramento do they continue to live a dusty pretence of life. The most popular foreign painters of the eighties and nineties also, the masters of The Hague and the Swedish artist Zorn, have lost much of their glamour; where they are still exhibited—at Toledo, Brooklyn, etc.— it is easy to see what were the reasons for their popularity and what were their weaknesses, how they relied on a compromise of tendencies, which French nineteenth-century painting elaborated with infinitely more consequence. For this very reason the latter encountered greater difficulties; its first organized appearance in America, the exhibition of Impressionists arranged in 1885 by Durand-Ruel, excited just as much opposition as the first collective appearance of the Post-Impressionists a generation later at the Armory Exhibition in 1913. We are concerned only with the crushing of the first resistance. All the American museums and private collections prove that French nineteenth-century painting is the only non-American modern school to have won for itself the right of citizenship in America. From Corot and Millet through the leaders of the Impressionists, Manet, Monet, Degas, Renoir, down to Cézanne, Seurat, Van Gogh and Gauguin, runs a chain so brilliant that these artists cannot be thoroughly studied without a knowledge of American collections. They belong together to the classical heritage of European painting, of which America with astounding energy has acquired a valuable portion, thus fulfilling a prophecy which Benjamin Franklin made in a letter to Charles Wilson Peale dated July 4, 1771: "The arts have always migrated westwards; and there is no doubt that later they will blossom on our side of the Atlantic, as soon as the number of prosperous inhabitants increases who are able and correspondingly willing to pay for them."

The illustrations in this volume, which despite its title is limited to the United States, represent an attempt to make this blossoming of art, so far as it is expressed by the ownership of European pictures down to the end of the nineteenth century, accessible to a wider circle of readers; we have followed no critical standard and refrained from making our own attributions, merely endeavouring to give a true picture of America's art treasures. The achievement of this aim was rendered difficult by both internal and external circumstances. Certain collections were inaccessible or undergoing alterations at the time when the editor visited America, and this made it advisable to exclude them, for the moment, from a representation of America's permanent treasury of art; on the other hand, our endeavour to reproduce the most celebrated pictures which have gone to America was often in conflict with our desire to include as much unknown material as possible; we wished, too, to include less important artists as well as the great masters; and lastly we wanted as many collections as possible to be represented in this book. All these different aims have resulted in a compromise, which may nevertheless serve to give an idea of the merits and demerits of American art-collecting. Great importance has been attached to the conception of national ownership of art. For this reason we have given the preference to public or semi-public collections, selecting among the private collections mainly those whose ultimate destination or accessibility entitles them to be considered as forming a part of what actually belongs to the nation. Collections of which the permanent existence seems doubtful have not been included, and we have also omitted works at present belonging to dealers, despite the fact that the latter have a number of very important works in their possession which will in all probability find a permanent resting-place in the United States. Another principle we followed was that of selecting almost without exception those pictures the originals of which we had had an opportunity of examining personally; the fact that in pictures characteristics are sometimes lacking which they appear to show in cleverly made photographic reproductions, is responsible for the absence from this volume of a few pictures which are believed to be among America's greatest art treasures owing to the fame they have achieved in photographs. Lastly, a selection such as this is bound to be somewhat subjective; it reproduces the picture of American art-collections which the editor has formed after long and careful study.

That this study could be utilized for the purposes of this book is due first of all to the great kindness of the directors of the museums and the owners of the private collections in question. To thank all to whom he is indebted would mean repeating the index of the book; the editor therefore limits himself to expressing his deepest gratitude for the help of all kinds accorded to him in general, and to Lord Duveen in particular, who lightened the editor's task, as he has done that of so many European scholars, by obtaining permission to visit private collections and procuring valuable photographic material.

THE PLATES

CATALAN SCHOOL, MIDDLE OR SECOND HALF OF 12TH CENTURY: Apse fresco from Santa Maria de Mur
Boston, Museum of Fine Arts

MASTER OF THE ST. GEORGE, EARLY 15TH CENTURY: St. George
Chicago, Art Institute

CATALAN SCHOOL, 15TH CENTURY: St. Martin
Boston, Museum of Fine Arts

BARTOLOMÉ BERMEJO: St. Engracia. About 1477
Boston, Isabella Stewart Gardner Museum

EL GRECO: Assumption of the Virgin
Chicago, Art Institute

EL GRECO: St. Martin. About 1598
Elkins Park, Joseph Widener Collection

EL GRECO: Madonna with the Child and Saints. About 1598
Elkins Park, Joseph Widener Collection

EL GRECO: Fray Hortensio Felix Paravicini. 1609
Boston, Museum of Fine Arts

EL GRECO: Cardinal Don Fernando Nino de Guevara. 1596—1600
New York, Metropolitan Museum

EL GRECO: Toledo during a thunderstorm. About 1600
New York, Metropolitan Museum

EL GRECO: Female Portrait. About 1600
Philadelphia, John G. Johnson Collection

VELÁZQUEZ: Luis de Gongora, 1622
Boston, Museum of Fine Arts

VELÁZQUEZ: Portrait of a Man. About 1623
Detroit, Institute of Art

VELÁZQUEZ: Don Balthasar Garlos and his Dwarf. About 1631
Boston, Museum of Fine Arts

VELÁZQUEZ: King Philip IV of Spain. 1644
New York, Frick Collection

ZURBARÁN: A Doctor of Salamanca University. About 1636
Boston, Isabella Stewart Gardner Museum

MURILLO: Don Andrea de Andrade y Col. 1650—60
New York, Metropolitan Museum

ZURBARÁN: Return of the Holy Family from Egypt. About 1638
Toledo (Ohio), Museum of Art

MURILLO: St. Thomas of Villanueva as a Child, giving away his clothes. 1670
Cincinnati, Art Museum

MURILLO: Girl with her Duenna at a window. 1665—75
Elkins Park, Joseph Widener Collection

GOYA: Women on a balcony. 1810—15
New York, Metropolitan Museum

GOYA: The Duchesse of Alba. 1797
New York, The Hispanic Society of America

GOYA: Queen Maria Luisa of Spain. 1790—92
New York, Metropolitan Museum

GOYA: Bullfight. About 1810
Toledo (Ohio), Museum of Art

GOYA: Imaginary City on a rock. 1815—18
New York, Metropolitan Museum

El Yll.mo Señor D.n Fr. Miguel Fernandez Obispo de Marcopolis, Administrador Apostolico de Quito.

GOYA: Fray Miguel Fernandez, Bishop of Marcopolis. 1815
Worcester (Mass.), Art Museum

GOYA: Don Sebastian Martinez. 1792
New York, Metropolitan Museum

GOYA: Gallants and a girl. About 1780
New York, S. Kress Collection

ITALO-BYZANTINE SCHOOL, LAST QUARTER OF 13TH CENTURY: The Last Judgement
Worcester (Mass.), Art Museum

DUCCIO: The Calling of the Apostles Peter and Andrew. About 1308—11
New York, S. Kress Collection

DUCCIO: The Temptation of Christ. About 1308—11
New York, Frick Collection

BERNARDINO DADDI: Vision of St. Dominic. 1338
New Haven, Yale University, Art Museum

GIOVANNI BARONZIO: Adoration of the Magi. About 1344—45
New York, Mogmar Art Foundation

PIETRO LORENZETTI: Madonna Enthroned with the Child. About 1340
Philadelphia, John G. Johnson Collection

GIOTTO: Presentation in the Temple. About 1320
Boston, Isabella Stewart Gardner Museum

PAOLO VENEZIANO: St. Maria Egyptiaca. About 1340
Worcester (Mass.), Art Museum

SASSETTA: St. Anthony assailed by Demons. About 1420—30
New Haven, Yale University, Art Museum

SASSETTA: The Journey of the Three Magi. About 1430
New York, Maitland Griggs Collection

GIOVANNI DI PAOLO: Adam and Eve driven out of the Garden of Eden. About 1450
New York, Philip Lehmann Collection

GIOVANNI DI PAOLO: John de Baptist in the Wilderness. About 1470
Chicago, Art Institute

GIOVANNI DI PAOLO: Salome bringing the head of John the Baptist on a charger
Chicago, Art Institute

STEFANO DA ZEVIO: The Virgin amidst rose-bushes. Early 15th century
Worcester (Mass.), Art Museum

MASOLINO: Annunciation. About 1430—40
Washington, Museum

MASOLINO: Crucifixion. About 1420
New York, Maitland Griggs Collection

MASACCIO: Young Man with turban. About 1427—29
Boston, Isabella Stewart Gardner Museum

PAOLO UCCELLO: Portrait of a Young Lady. Middle of 15th century
Boston, Isabella Stewart Gardner Museum

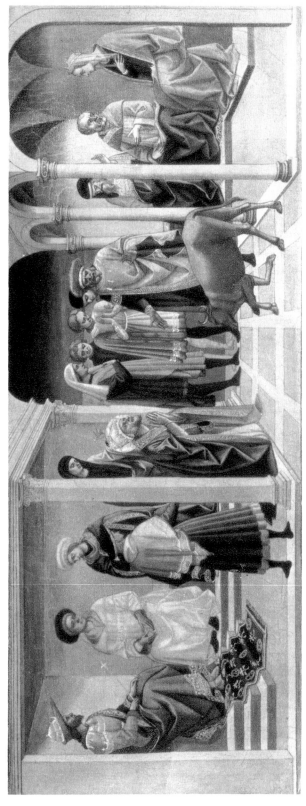

FRANCESCO PESELLINO: Miracle of St. Sylvester. Middle of 15th century
Worcester (Mass.), Art Museum

ANTONIO POLLAIUOLO: The Rape of Dejanira. About 1480
New Haven, Yale University, Art Museum

PIERO POLLAIUOLO: Portrait of a Young Lady. About 1480
Boston, Isabella Stewart Gardner Museum

ANDREA CASTAGNO: Portrait of a Young Man. About 1445—50
New York, Pierpont Morgan Library

ANDREA CASTAGNO: The Youthful David. About 1450
Elkins Park, Joseph Widener Collection

COSIMO TURA: Adoration of the Magi. About 1480
Cambridge (Mass.), Fogg Art Museum

COLANTONIO: Male Portrait. About 1450
Cleveland, Museum of Art

BOTTICELLI: Lorenzo Lorenzano. About 1490
Philadelphia, John G. Johnson Collection

BOTTICELLI: Communion of St. Jerome. About 1490
New York, Metropolitan Museum

BOTTICELLI: Madonna of the Eucharist. About 1470
Boston, Isabella Stewart Gardner Museum

BOTTICELLI. *Adoration of the Magi.* About 1472–73.

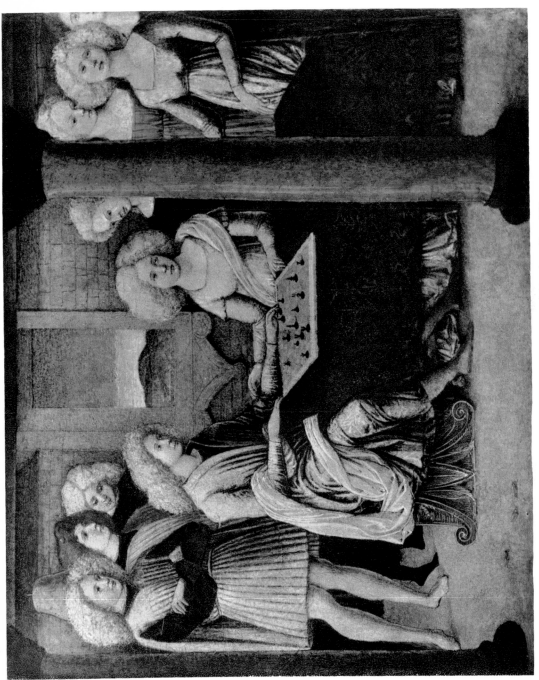

FRANCESCO DI GIORGIO: Young Couple plaining chess. About 1490
New York, Maitland Griggs Collection

DOMENICO GHIRLANDAIO: Young Woman. About 1490
New Haven, Yale University, Art Museum

LORENZO DI CREDI: Self-portrait. 1488
Elkins Park, Joseph Widener Collection

FRA BARTOLOMEO: The Virgin with the Child and Saints
New York, Metropolitan Museum

LUCA SIGNORELLI: Virgin and Child. About 1510
New York, Jules Bache Collection

FILIPPINO LIPPI: Adoration of the Child. About 1480
Toledo (Ohio), Museum of Art

FILIPPINO LIPPI: The Holy Family with St. John and St. Margaret. 1497
Cleveland, Museum of Art

BARTOLOMEO VIVARINI: Virgin and Child. 1472
New York, Metropolitan Museum

ANDREA MANTEGNA: St. Jerome. About 1450
Washington, Museum

ANDREA MANTEGNA: Tarquin and the Sibyl. End of 15th century
Cincinnati, Art Museum

ANDREA MANTEGNA: Judith. About 1490
Elkins Park, Joseph Widener Collection

ANTONELLO DA MESSINA: Head of a Youth. About 1470
New York, Metropolitan Museum

GIOVANNI BELLINI: Portrait of a Youth. End of 15th century.
Elkins Park, Joseph Widener Collection

JACOPO DA VALENCIA: St. Jerome. About 1500
Boston, Museum of Fine Arts

CARLO CRIVELLI: Pietà. 1485
Boston, Museum of Fine Arts

GENTILE BELLINI: A Turkish Painter. 1479—80
Boston, Isabella Stewart Gardner Museum

JACOPO DE' BARBARI: Lovers of unequal age. 1503
Philadelphia, John G. Johnson Collection

GIOVANNI BELLINI: St. Francis in landscape. About 1840
New York, Frick Art Museum

GIOVANNI BELLINI: Bacchanal. 1514
Elkins Park, Joseph Widener Collection

Italy

VITTORE CARPACCIO: Meditation on the Passion of Christ. About 1510
New York, Metropolitan Museum

CIMA DA CONEGLIANO: Silenus. About 1500
Philadelphia, John G. Johnson Collection

RAPHAEL: Mourning for Christ. 1504—5
Boston, Isabella Stewart Gardner Museum

RAPHAEL: Christ on the Mount of Olives. 1504—5
New York, Metropolitan Museum

RAPHAEL: The Colonna Altar-piece. 1504—5
New York, Metropolitan Museum

RAPHAEL: The small Cowper Madonna. About 1505
Elkins Park, Joseph Widener Collection

RAPHAEL: The Alba Madonna. About 1508
Washington, Museum

RAPHAEL: Count Tommaso Inghirami. About 1512-14
Boston, Isabella Stewart Gardner Museum

TITIAN: Portrait of a Man. About 1510
New York, Samuel H. Kress Collection

GIORGIONE: Adoration of the Shepherds. About 1505

TITIAN: Venus with the Flute-player. About 1560
New York, Metropolitan Museum

BARTOLOMEO VENETO: Portrait of a Man. About 1510
New York, Samuel H. Kress Collection

PALMA VECCHIO: Portrait of a Bearded Man. About 1510
Philadelphia, John G. Johnson Collection

SEBASTIANO DEL PIOMBO: Christopher Columbus. 1519
New York, Metropolitan Museum

TITIAN: Man with a Falcon. About 1530
New York, Erickson Collection

TITIAN: Venus with the Mirror. About 1555.
Washington, Museum

TITIAN: Rape of Europa. About 1560
Boston, Isabella Stewart Gardner Museum

TITIAN: Nicolas Perrenot Granvella. About 1548
Kansas City, William R. Nelson Gallery of Art

LORENZO LOTTO: St. Peter Martyr. 1549
Cambridge (Mass.), Fogg Art Museum

G. B. MORONI: Portrait of a Scholar. About 1570
Elkins Park, Joseph Widener Collection

G. B. MORONI: The Captain of Bergamo. About 1560
Worcester (Mass.), Art Museum

G. B. MORONI: Portrait of a Priest. About 1560
Minneapolis, Institute of Arts

LVCRETIA NOBILISS. ALEXIS ALARDI
BERGOMENSIS FILIA HONORATISS.
FRANCISCI CATANEI VERTVATIS
VXOR DIVAE ANNAE ALBINENSE
TEMPLVM IPSA STATVENDV CVRAVIT.
M. D. LVII.

G. B. MORONI: The Prioress Lucrezia Cattaneo. 1557
New York, Metropolitan Museum

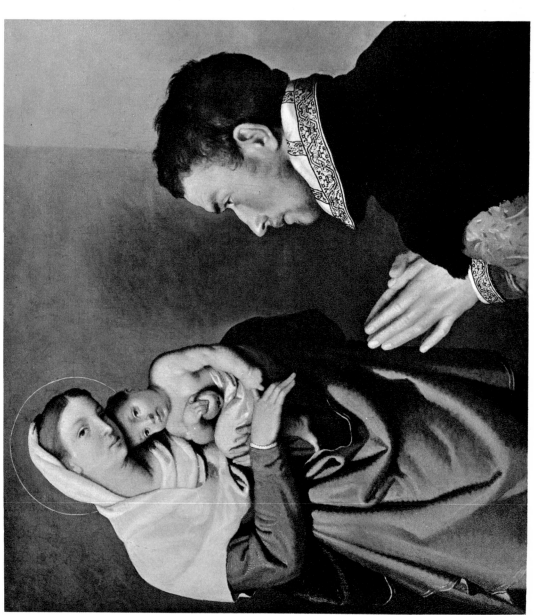

G. B. MORONI: Madonna with praying Donor. About 1560
New York, Sam. H. Kress Collection

SAVOLDO: St. Matthew and the Angel
New York, Metropolitan Museum

Italy

TINTORETTO: St. Peter walking on the sea. About 1540
New York, G. L. Winthrop Collection

TINTORETTO: Baptism of Christ. 1562—68
New York, Arthur Sachs Collection, on loan to the Fogg Art Museum, Cambridge (Mass.)

PARIS BORDONE: Adoration of the Magi. About 1550

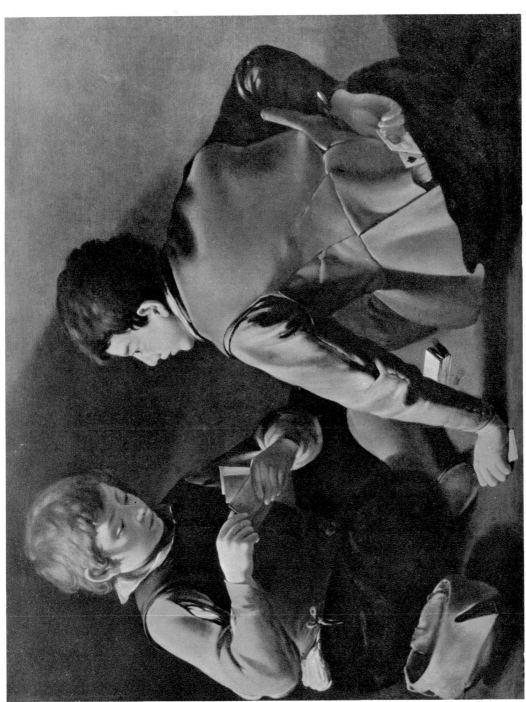

CARAVAGGIO: Card-players. 1595—1600
Cambridge (Mass.), Fogg Art Museum

TINTORETTO: Lady in black. About 1578
Boston, Isabella Stewart Gardner Museum

BERNARDINO LUINI: Portrait of a Lady. About 1515
Washington, Andrew W. Mellon Collection

PAOLO VERONESE: A Lady with her Daughter
Baltimore, Walters Art Gallery

PAOLO VERONESE: Mars and Venus. About 1580
New York, Metropolitan Museum

CORREGGIO: Four Saints. About 1515
New York, Metropolitan Museum

DOSSO DOSSI: The Three Ages of Man
New York, Metropolitan Museum

DOMENICO BECCAFUMI: Portrait of a Gentleman. About 1530
St. Louis, City Art Museum

RIDOLFO GHIRLANDAIO: A Florentine Nobleman. About 1520
Chicago, Art Institute

PONTORMO: The Halberdier. About 1528—30
New York, Metropolitan Museum

BACCIO BANDINELLI: Self-portrait. About 1530
Boston, Isabella Stewart Gardner Museum

BERNARDO STROZZI: St. Catherine. About 1620
Hartford, Wadsworth Atheneum

G. B. TIEPOLO: Portrait of a Lady. 1762—70
Cleveland: Henry G. Dalton Collection

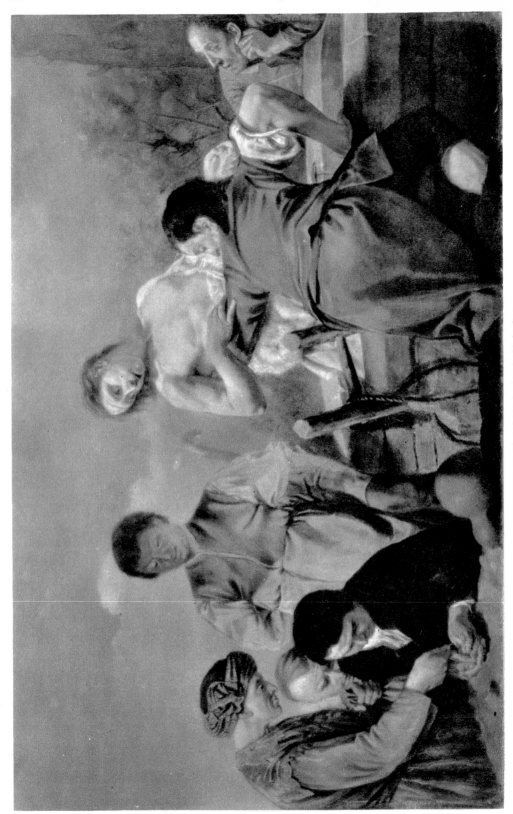

PIAZZETTA: Joseph sold into bondage by his brethren
New York, Metropolitan Museum

G. B. TIEPOLO: Rinaldo bewitched by Armida. About 1740
Chicago, Art Institute

ALESSANDRO MAGNASCO: The Synagogue. About 1730
Cleveland Museum of Art

G. P. PANNINI: Sketch for the "Piazza Navona"
Chicago, Art Institute

a) PIETRO LONGHI: The pretended fainting-fit

b) PIETRO LONGHI: Blind-man's-buff

New York, Samuel H. Kress Collection

FRANCESCO GUARDI: Festival on the Grand Canal
Philadelphia, John G. Johnson Collection

FRANCESCO GUARDI: The Rialto
Elkins Park, Joseph Widener Collection

JAN VAN EYCK: St. Francis receiving the Stigmata. About 1438
Philadelphia, John G. Johnson Collection

PETRUS CHRISTUS: St. Eligius. **1449**
New York, Philip Lehmann Collection

PETRUS CHRISTUS: Annunciation
New York, Metropolitan Museum

JAN VAN EYCK: Annunciation About 1434
Washington, Museum

PETRUS CHRISTUS: Portrait of a Carthusian Monk. 1466
New York, Jules S. Bache Collection

ROGIER VAN DER WEYDEN: St. Luke painting the Virgin. About 1450
Boston, Museum of Fine Arts

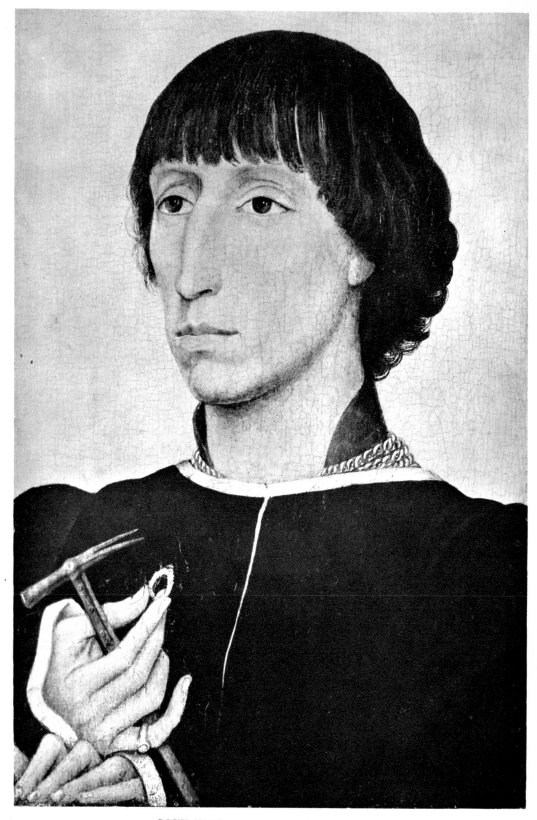

ROGIER VAN DER WEYDEN: Meliaduse d'Este. 1450
New York, Metropolitan Museum

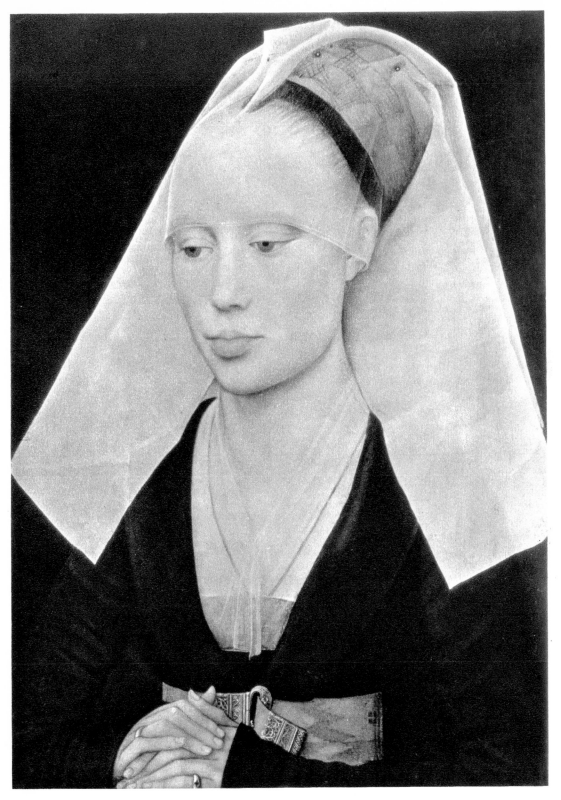

ROGIER VAN DER WEYDEN: Portrait of a Young Woman. About 1455
Washington, Museum

DIRK BOUTS: Portrait of a Man. About 1470
New York, Metropolitan Museum

DIRK BOUTS: Moses and the Burning Bush. About 1465
Philadelphia, John G. Johnson Collection

HUGO VAN DER GOES: Portrait of a praying Man. About 1470
New York, Metropolitan Museum

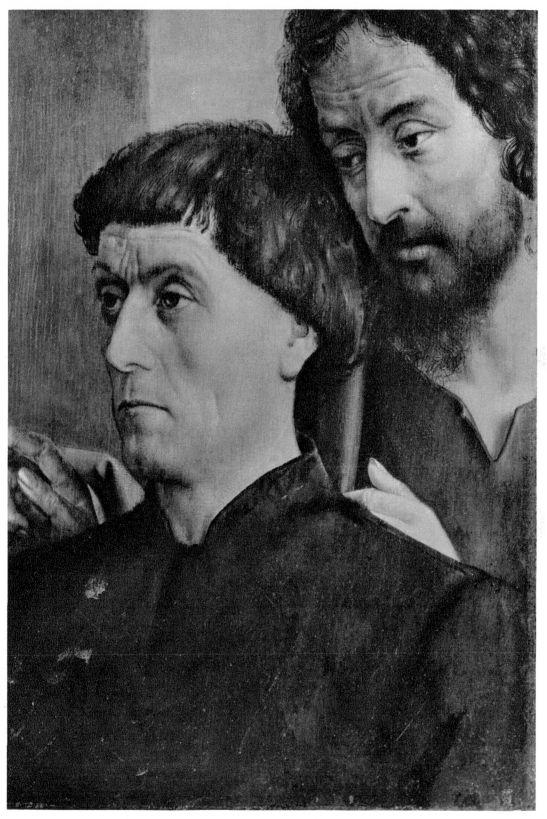

HUGO VAN DER GOES: Portrait of a Donor with John the Baptist. About 1480
Baltimore, Walters Art Gallery

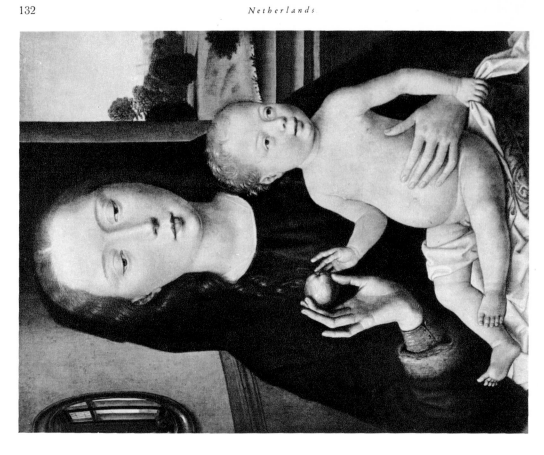

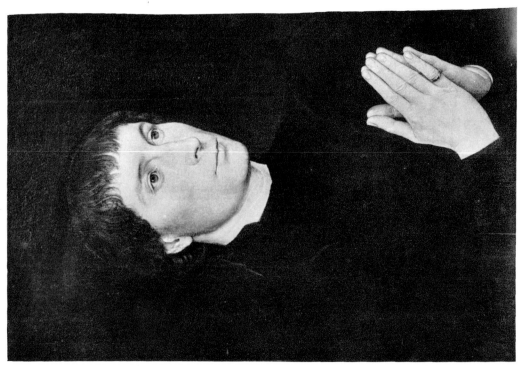

HANS MEMLING: Thomas Portinari. About 1472
New York, Metropolitan Museum

JUSTUS OF GHENT: Adoration of the Magi. 1466
New York, George Blumenthal Collection

MASTER OF THE VIRGO INTER VIRGINES: Mourning for the Dead Christ. Last quarter of 15th century
New York, Metropolitan Museum

HANS MEMLING: The Virgin with the Child and two Angels. About 1480
Washington, Museum

MASTER OF THE ST. LUCY LEGEND: The Virgin with female Saints in a rose-garden. About 1489
Detroit, Institute of Art

GERARD DAVID: Mourning for Christ beneath the Cross. About 1510
Philadelphia, John G. Johnson Collection

HIERONYMUS BOSCH: The Mocking of Christ. About 1500
Philadelphia, John G. Johnson Collection

HIERONYMUS BOSCH: Adoration of the Magi. End of 15th century
New York, Metropolitan Museum

QUENTIN MASSYS: Bust-portrait of a Woman. 1520—30
New York, Metropolitan Museum

QUENTIN MASSYS: Man with a pink. 1510—20
Chicago, Art Institute

QUENTIN MASSYS: St. Mary Egyptiaca. About 1500

QUENTIN MASSYS: St. Mary Magdalen. About 1500   *Philadelphia, John G. Johnson Collection*

JOACHIM PATINIR: Rest on the Flight into Egypt. About 1520
Minneapolis, Institute of Arts

JOACHIM PATINIR: Assumption of the Virgin. About 1515—20
Philadelphia, John G. Johnson Collection

BERNARD VAN ORLEY: Virgin and Child. About 1513
New York, Metropolitan Museum

LUCAS VAN LEYDEN: Adoration of the Magi. About 1510
Chicago, Art Institute

PIETER BRUEGHEL THE ELDER: Open-air Wedding Dance. 1566
Detroit, Institute of Art

PIETER BRUEGHEL THE ELDER: Harvest. 1565
New York, Metropolitan Museum

PIETER BRUEGHEL THE ELDER: The unfaithful Shepherd. About 1568
Philadelphia, John G. Johnson Collection

HEMESSEN: "Take up thy bed and walk!" Middle of 16th century
New York, Chester Dale Colection

MABUSE: Anna van Bergen, Marquise de Veere. About 1520
Boston, Isabella Stewart Gardner Museum

RUBENS: Count Heinrich von Bergh. About 1630
Boston, Isabella Stewart Gardner Museum

MARYE the QUEENE

ANTONIS MOR: Queen Mary of England. About 1554
Boston, Isabella Stewart Gardner Museum

RUBENS: Samson and Delilah. About 1615
Chicago, Art Institute

RUBENS: Wolf and Fox Hunt 1617
New York, Metropolitan Museum

VAN DYCK: Paola Adorno - Brignole Sale. About 1625
Elkins Park, Joseph Widener Collection

VAN DYCK: Marchesa Elena Grimaldi-Cattaneo. 1623
Elkins Park, Joseph Widener Collection

VAN DYCK: Helena Tromper-Dubois. About 1631
Chicago, Art Institute

VAN DYCK: James Stuart, Duke of Lennox. About 1640
New York, Metropolitan Museum

JAN LYS: The Satyr and the Peasant. About 1625
Elkins Park, Joseph Widener Collection

FRANS HALS: Flute-player. About 1629—30
Toledo (Ohio), Museum of Art

FRANS HALS: Fishergirl. About 1635
Brooklin, Museum of Art

CORNELIS DE VOS: Mother and Children. About 1630
New York, Metropolitan Museum

FRANS HALS: Jonkheer Ramp and his Mistress. 1623
New York, Metropolitan Museum

FRANS HALS: Portrait of a Gentleman. About 1650
Elkins Park, Joseph Widener Collection

FRANS HALS: Michael de Wael. About 1634
Cincinnati, Taft Museum

FRANS HALS: Woman with prayer-book. 1648
Boston, Museum of Fine Arts

REMBRANDT: Man holding a letter. About 1662
Elkins Park, Joseph Widener Collection

REMBRANDT: Portrait of a Man. 1637
Washington, Corcoran Gallery

REMBRANDT: Portrait of a Married Couple. 1633
Boston, Isabella Stewart Gardner Museum

REMBRANDT: Landscape with Obelisk. 1638
Boston, Isabella Stewart Gardner Museum

REMBRANDT: Polish Horseman. About 1655
New York, Frick Art Museum

REMBRANDT: Self-portrait. 1658
New York, Frick Art Museum

REMBRANDT: Lucretia. 1666
Minneapolis, Institute of Arts

REMBRANDT: Girl behind a door. 1645
Chicago, Art Institute

REMBRANDT: Magdalena van Loo. About 1668
Elkins Park, Joseph Widener Collection

REMBRANDT: St. Bartholomew
New York, Mrs. Henry Goldman Collection

REMBRANDT: Aristotle. 1653
New York, Erickson Collection

REMBRANDT: Pilate washing his hands. About 1665
New York, Metropolitan Museum

REMBRANDT: The Mill. About 1650
Elkins Park, Joseph Widener Collection

REMBRANDT: Old Woman cutting her nails. 1658
New York, Metropolitan Museum

FERDINAND BOL: Girl at the window. 1663
Toledo (Ohio), Museum of Art

JAN STEEN: Moses bringing forth water from the rock. About 1660
Philadelphia, John G. Johnson Collection

PIETER DE HOOCH· Skittles-players. 1665—68
St. Louis, City Art Museum

PIETER DE HOOCH: Woman and Child in a courtyard. About 1656
Elkins Park, Joseph Widener Collection

JAN VERMEER: Young Woman with water-jug. About 1665
New York, Metropolitan Museum

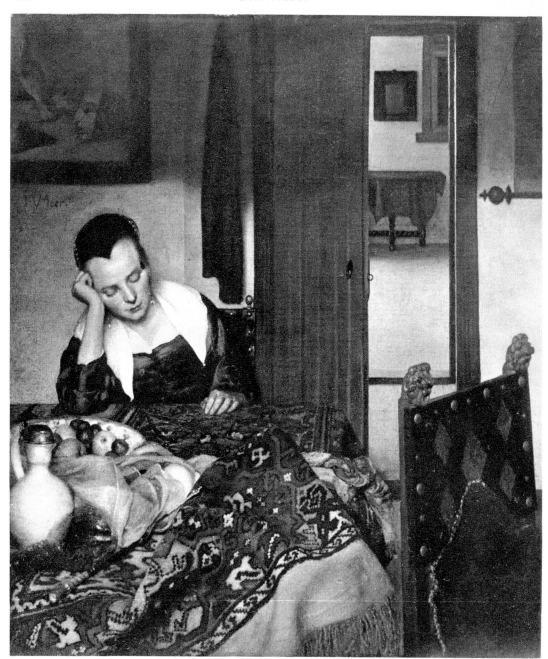

JAN VERMEER; Sleeping Girl. About 1658
New York, Metropolitan Museum

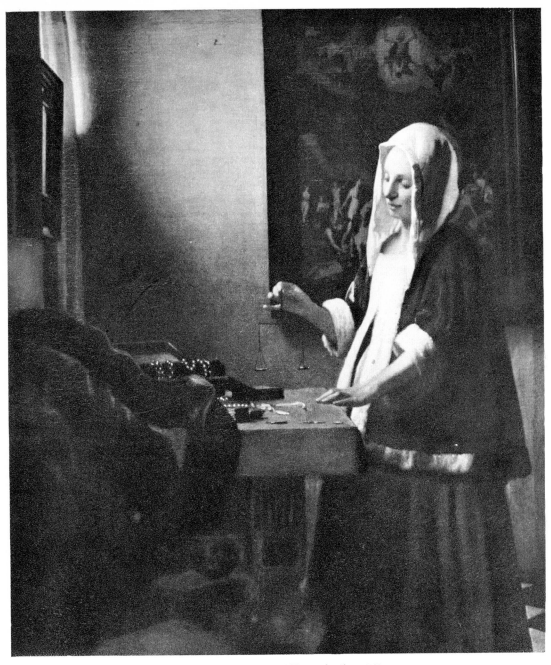

JAN VERMEER: Woman weighing pearls. About 1665
Elkins Park, Joseph Widener Collection

JAN VERMEER: Lace-maker. About 1660
Washington, Museum

JAN VERMEER: Girl with flute. About 1670
Elkins Park, Joseph Widener Collection

JAN VERMEER: Smiling Girl. About 1670
Washington, Museum

AERT DE GELDER: Girl. About 1690
Chicago, Art Institute

JACOB VAN RUYSDAEL: Forest Landscape. About 1660—65
Elkins Park, Joseph Widener Collection

JACOB VAN RUYSDAEL: Wheatfields
New York, Metropolitan Museum

13

HOBBEMA: Landscape with Cottages. 1663
Washington, Museum

CONRAD VON SOEST: Coronation of the Virgin. Early 15th century
Cleveland, Museum of Art

JOHANN KOERBECKE: Annunciation. 1457
Chicago, Art Institute

MASTER OF THE AUGSBURG VISITATION ; Crucifixion. About 1480—85
Detroit, Institute of Art

MASTER OF ULM: A Pair of Lovers. About 1470
Cleveland, Museum of Art

FRANCONIAN SCHOOL: Portrait of a Young Man. 1491
New York, Metropolitan Museum

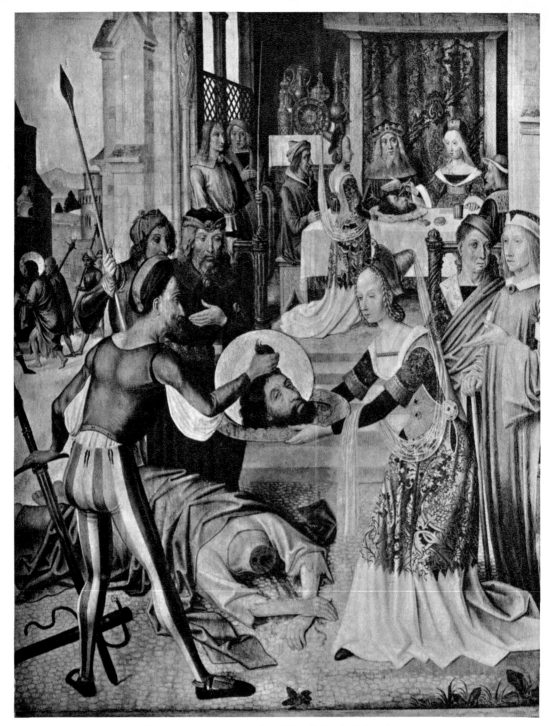

MASTER OF ST. SEVERIN; Beheading of John the Baptist. Early 16th century
Boston, Museum of Fine Arts

ALBRECHT DÜRER: St. Anne with the Virgin and Child. 1519
New York, Metropolitan Museum

ALBRECHT DÜRER: Portrait of a Young Man. 1504
Indianapolis, G. H. A. Clowes Collection

ALBRECHT DÜRER: Portrait of a Young Man. 1507
Washington, Museum

LUCAS CRANACH: Young Man with a rosary. About 1510—12
New York, Metropolitan Museum

LUCAS CRANACH: Portrait of a Young Lady. About 1540
New York, John Schiff Collection

HANS VON KULMBACH: Girl at a window. 1508
New York, Metropolitan Museum

LUCAS CRANACH: The Judgement of Paris. About 1530
St. Louis, City Art Museum

CHRISTOPH AMBERGER: Portrait of an elderly Man. About 1550
Chicago, Art Institute

HANS MALER; Ulrich Fugger. 1525
New York, Metropolitan Museum

BARTEL BEHAM: Leonhard von Eck. 1527
New York, Metropolitan Museum

ETATIS ANNOR· 25
·1507·

IOHANES BVRGKMAIR
PINGEBAT IN AVGVSTA
AS RECIA

HANS BURGKMAIR: Portrait of an Architect. 1507
New York, Ernst Rosenfeld Collection

MASTER OF THE ANGERER PORTRAITS: Clean-shaven Man. Early 16th century
St. Louis, City Art Museum

HANS HOLBEIN THE YOUNGER: Benedikt von Hertenstein. 1517
New York, Metropolitan Museum

HANS HOLBEIN THE YOUNGER: Lady Elisabeth Rich. About 1540
New York, Metropolitan Museum

ANNO ÆTATIS · SVE · LVII ·

HANS HOLBEIN THE YOUNGER; Lady Margaret Butts. 1541—43
Boston, Isabella Stewart Gardner Museum

HANS HOLBEIN THE YOUNGER: Dirk Berck 1536
Washington, Andrew W. Mellon Collection

ALBRECHT DÜRER: Portrait of a Man. 1521
Boston, Isabella Stewart Gardner Museum

STYLE OF MARCUS GHEERAERTS THE YOUNGER; Lady and Child. 1598
Providence, Rhode Island School of Design

HOGARTH: Lady and Child. Middle of 18th century
Washington, Corcoran Gallery of Art

HOGARTH: Mr. and Mrs. William James. 1744
Worcester (Mass.), Art Museum

HOGARTH: The Price Family. Middle of 18th century
New York, Metropolitan Museum

JOSEPH HIGHMORE: Portrait of a Gentleman
San Marino (California), Huntington Art Gallery

GAINSBOROUGH: Mrs. Mary Graham. 1775—76
Elkins Park, Joseph Widener Collection

GAINSBOROUGH: The Artist's Daughter Margaret. 1757—58
New York, Metropolitan Museum

GAINSBOROUGH; The Artist's Daughters Margaret and Mary. About 1765
Worcester (Mass.), Art Museum

REYNOLDS: Theresa Parker. 1787
San Marino (California), Huntington Art Gallery

GAINSBOROUGH: The Blue Boy. About 1770
San Marino (California), Huntington Art Gallery

REYNOLDS: Nancy Parsons, Viscountess Maynard. 1769
New York, Jules S. Bache Collection

ROMNEY: Mrs. Charlotte Davenport. 1777
Washington, Museum

REYNOLDS: Lady Diana Crosbie. 1777
San Marino (California), Huntington Art Gallery

REYNOLDS: Mrs. Siddons as the Tragic Muse. 1784
San Marino (California), Huntington Art Gallery

RAEBURN: The Elphinstone Children. About 1800
Cincinnati, Art Museum

JOHN HOPPNER: The Artist's Three Children. 1799
Elkins Park, Joseph Widener Collection

THOMAS LAWRENCE: William Locke. 1790
Boston, Museum of Fine Arts

GAINSBOROUGH: The Cottage Door. 1776—78
San Marino (California), Huntington Art Gallery

JOHN CONSTABLE: Hampstead Heath
Philadelphia, Pennsylvania Museum of Art

JOHN CONSTABLE: Weymouth Bay
Boston, Museum of Fine Arts

RICHARD BONINGTON: Seacoast in Normandy. About 1825
Philadelphia, Pennsylvania Museum of Art

RICHARD BONINGTON: Santa Maria della Salute, Venice. About 1825
Worcester (Mass.), Art Museum

J. M. W. TURNER: The Grand Canal, Venice. About 1840
Baltimore, Walters Art Gallery

WILLIAM BLAKE: Christ and the Woman taken in adultery. About 1810
Boston, Museum of Fine Arts

SOUTHERN FRENCH SCHOOL: The Virgin and Child, with the Blessed Peter of Luxembourg presenting a Donor. About 1400
Worcester (Mass.), Art Museum

SOUTHERN FRENCH SCHOOL: A Bishop-Saint with Donor. Early 15th century
Cleveland, Museum of Art

SOUTHERN FRENCH SCHOOL: St. Jerome translating the Gospels. Middle of 15th century
New York, Mogmar Art Foundation

NORTHERN FRENCH SCHOOL: Mourning for the Body of Christ. About 1460
Chicago, Max Epstein Collection

SIMON MARMION: St. Jerome with a Donor. About 1460
Philadelphia, John G. Johnson Collection

BURGUNDIAN SCHOOL: The Grand Bastard of Burgundy with a Bishop-Saint. About 1500
Worcester (Mass.), Art Museum

THE MASTER OF MOULINS: Portrait of a Man praying. About 1500
New York, Ernst Rosenfeld Collection

FONTAINEBLEAU SCHOOL: Diane de Poitiers. About 1560
Worcester (Mass.), Art Museum

France

LOUIS LENAIN: Peasants in Landscape. 1630—40
Hartford, Wadsworth Atheneum

FRENCH SCHOOL: Portrait of a unknown Lady. About 1660
New York, G. L. Winthrop Collection

PIERRE DUBORDIEU: Portrait of a Young Woman. About 1640
Chicago, Art Institute

NICOLAS POUSSIN: Triumph of Neptune and Amphitrite. 1639
Philadelphia, Pennsylvania Museum of Art

NICOLAS POUSSIN: Blind Orion seeking the rising sun. 1638
New York, Metropolitan Museum

NICOLAS DE LARGILLIÈRE: The Marquis de Montespan. About 1700
San Francisco, Palace of the Legion of Honour

ANTOINE WATTEAU: "Mezzetin". 1716—18
New York, Metropolitan Museum

NICOLAS LANCRET: The Dancer Camargo. About 1730
Washington, Museum

CHARDIN: Man blowing bubbles. About 1740
Kansas City, William R. Nelson Gallery of Art

F. H. DROUAIS: Madame d'Aiguirande. About 1750
Cleveland, John L. Severance Collection

MAURICE QUENTIN DE LA TOUR: Madame de Mondonville. 1747
St. Louis, City Art Museum

JEAN FRAGONARD: The Rendezvous. 1770—72
New York, Frick Art Museum

JEAN FRAGONARD: The Love-letter. About 1760
New York, Jules S. Bache Collection

LOUIS DAVID: Mademoiselle Charlotte du Val d'Ognes. About 1795
New York, Metropolitan Museum

JEAN INGRES: Portrait of a Gentleman. About 1813
New York, Metropolitan Museum

GÉRICAULT: Horseman at the door of an inn. About 1820
New York, G. L. Winthrop Collection

GÉRICAULT: Hercules killing Licas. About 1820
Northampton, Smith College, Museum of Art

DELACROIX: Lion-haut. 1801
Chicago, Art Institute

DELACROIX: Paganini. About 1830
Washington, Phillips Memorial Gallery

DAUMIER: Madame Pipelet. About 1840
Providence, Rhode Island School of Design

DAUMIER: In the Third Class. About 1840
New York, Metropolitan Museum

DAUMIER: After the Theatre. About 1840
Kansas City, William R. Nelson Gallery of Art

DAUMIER: The Revolt. About 1848
Washington, Phillips Memorial Gallery

CHASSÉRIAU: Arabian Horsemen carrying away their dead. 1850
New York, G. L. Winthrop Collection

COURBET: The Stag-hunt. 1857
Boston, Museum of Fine Arts

COURBET: The Amazon (Madame Louise Colet). About 1856
New York, Metropolitan Museum

MILLET: Planting Potatoes. About 1860
Boston, Museum of Fine Arts

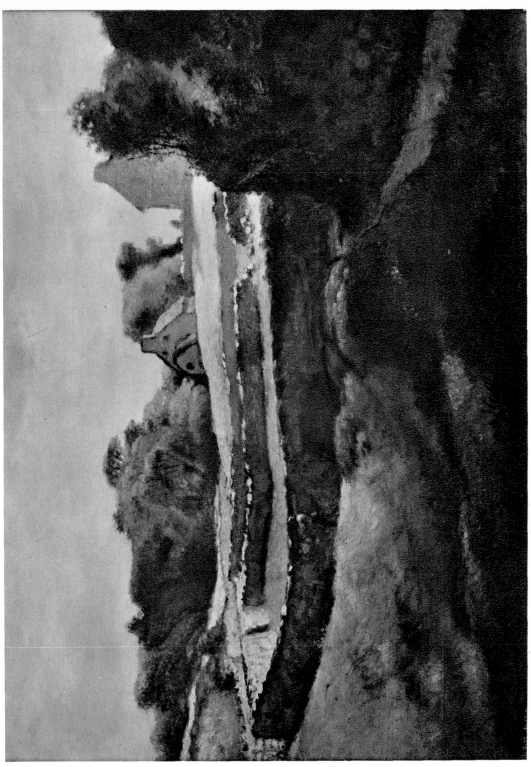

MILLET: Farm at Gréville. 1871
Northampton, Smith College, Museum of Art

COROT: Monsieur Abel Osmond. 1829
New York, Adolf Lewisohn Collection

COROT: Portrait of a Girl. 1859
New York, Chester Dale Collection

COROT: The Atelier. 1865—68
Elkins Park, Joseph Widener Collection

CHASSÉRIAU: The Fisherman's Wife. 1850
Providence, Rhode Island School of Design

COROT: The Church of Saint-Salvi, Albi. About 1830
Chicago, Art Institute

COROT: Wood-gatherers. About 1860
Washington, Corcoran Gallery of Art

MANET: Kneeling Monk. About 1865
Boston, Museum of Fine Arts

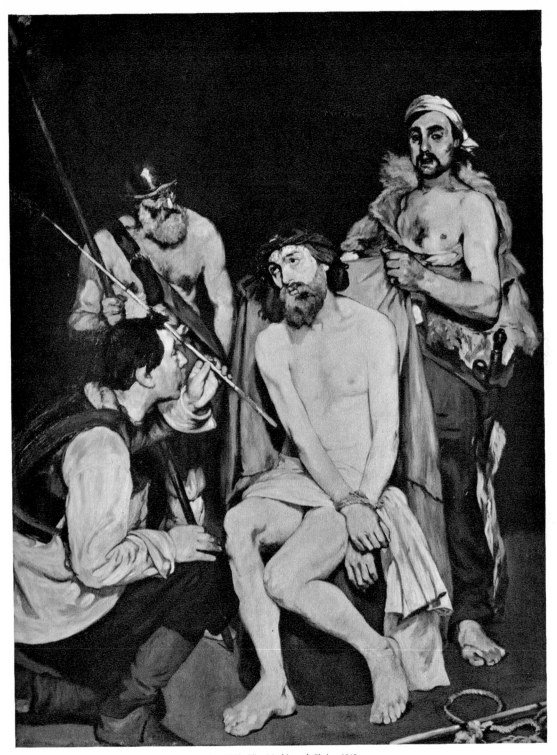

MANET: The Mocking of Christ. 1865
Chicago, Art Institute

MANET: The Son of Madame Lange. 1861
Chicago, Art Institute

MANET: Mademoiselle Victorine in Espada costume. 1862
New York, Metropolitan Museum

MANET: The dead Toreador. 1864
Elkins Park, Joseph Widener Collection

MANET: In the Boat. About 1874
New York, Metropolitan Museum

MONET: The Seine. 1870
New York, Adolf Lewisohn Collection

MONET: saint-Lazare Station. 1877
Chicago. Art Institute

DEGAS; Achille de Gas. 1856—57
New York, Chester Dale Collection

DEGAS: Madame Gaujelin. 1867
Boston, Isabella Stewart Gardner Museum

DEGAS: Carriage on the race-course. 1874
Boston, Museum of Fine Arts

DEGAS: Ballet-dancers practising. About 1870
New York, Metropolitan Museum

DEGAS: The Duke and Duchess de Morbilli. About 1870
Boston, Museum of Fine Arts

RENOIR: Madame Darras. 1871
New York, Adolf Lewisohn Collection

RENOIR: Woman sewing. 1879
Chicago, Art Institute

RENOIR; Odalisque. 1870
New York, Chester Dale Collection

RENOIR: Oarsmen at lunch. 1881
Washington, Phillips Memorial Gallery

CÉZANNE: Landscape near Aix-en-Provence. About 1890
New York, Metropolitan Museum

CÉZANNE: Card-players. 1892
Merion, Barnes Foundation

CÉZANNE: Youth in a small hat. 1885
New York, Chester Dale Collection

TOULOUSE-LAUTREC: Prostitute. About 1890
Merion, Barnes Foundation

VAN GOGH: La Mousmée. 1890
New York, Chester Dale Collection

VAN GOGH: The Arlésienne. 1888
New York, Adolf Lewisohn Collection

SEURAT: Sunday on the Island of Grande-Jatte. 1884—86
Chicago, Art Institute

SOURCES OF THE PHOTOGRAPHS

The pictures have been reproduced with the kind consent of the following:

Baltimore, Walters Art Gallery, Nos. 104, 131, 240

Boston, Museum of Fine Arts, Nos. 1, 3, 8, 12, 68, 69, 125, 166, 200, 234, 237, 241, 272, 273, 282, 292 a, 293

Boston, Isabella Stewart Gardner Museum, Nos. 4, 16, 33, 42, 43, 46, 53, 70, 76 a, 80, 89, 102, 111, 151, 152, 153, 169, 170, 215, 217, 291

Brooklyn, Museum of Art. No. 161 a

Cambrigde, Fogg Art Museum, Nos. 49, 91, 99, 101

Chicago, Art Institute, Nos. 2, 5, 37, 38, 109, 115, 117, 132 b, 141, 146, 154, 158, 174, 191, 196, 208, 245, 251 a, 265, 280, 283, 284, 289, 295, 304

Cincinnati, Art Museum, Nos. 19, 64, 232

Cincinnati, Taft Museum, No. 165

Cleveland, Museum of Art, Nos. 50, 61, 113, 116, 195, 198, 243, 258

Detroit, Institute of Art, Nos. 13, 136, 147, 197

Elkins Park, Mr. Joseph Widener, Nos. 6, 7, 20, 48, 57, 65, 67, 73, 78, 192, 119 b, 156, 157, 160, 164, 167, 175, 179, 184, 187, 189, 192, 223, 233, 278, 286

Hartford, Wadsworth Atheneum, Nos. 112, 250

Kansas City, William R. Nelson Gallery of Art, Nos. 90, 257, 269

Minneapolis, Institute of Arts, Nos. 94, 143, 173

New York, Metropolitan Museum, 9, 10, 17, 21, 23, 25, 27, 52, 58, 62, 66, 74, 76 b, 77, 83, 86, 95. 97, 105, 106, 107, 110, 114, 122, 126, 128, 130, 132 a, 134, 139, 140, 141, 148, 155, 159, 162, 163, 178, 180, 185, 186, 193, 199, 201, 204, 206, 209, 210, 213, 214, 221, 224, 253, 255, 262, 263, 268, 273, 285, 287, 292 b, 298

New York, The Hispanic Society of America, No. 22

New York, Frick Art Reference Library, Nos. 15, 30 b, 72, 171, 172, 260

New York, Pierpont Morgan Libray, No, 47

New York, Mr. George Blumenthal, No. 133

New York, Mr. Chester Dale, 150, 277, 290, 296, 300, 302

New York, Lord Duveen, Nos. 31 b, 59, 63, 87, 103, 124, 127, 135, 177, 188, 190, 194, 216, 228, 229, 244, 256, 261

New York, Mrs. Henry Goldmann, No. 176

New York, Mr. Maitland Griggs, Nos. 36 a, 41, 55

New York, Mr. Kress, Nos. 28, 30 a, 96, 118 a, 118 b

New York, Mr. Phil. Lehmann, Nos. 36 b, 121

New York, Morgan Photographs, Nos. 299, 301

New York, Mr. Ernst Rosenfeld, Nos. 211, 248

New York, Mr. John Schiff, No. 205

New York, Mr. G. L. Winthrop, Nos. 98, 100, 251 b, 264 b, 271

Northampton, Smith College, Museum of Art, No. 264 a

Philadelphia, Pennsylvania Museum of Art, No. 236, 238, 252

Philadelphia, John G. Johnson Collection, Nos. 11, 32, 51, 71, 75, 85, 119 a, 120, 129, 137, 138, 142 a, 142 b, 144, 149, 182, 246

Providence, Rhode Island School of Design, Nos. 218, 267, 279

San Francisco, Palace of the Legion of Honour, No. 254

San Marino, Huntington Art Gallery, Nos. 222, 226, 227, 230, 231, 235

St. Louis, City Art Museum, Nos. 108, 183, 207, 212, 259

Toledo, Museum of Art, Nos. 18, 24, 60, 161 b, 181

Washington, Corcoran Gallery, Nos. 168, 219, 281

Washington, Philips Memorial Gallery, Nos. 266, 270, 297

Worcester, Art Museum, Nos. 26, 29, 34, 39, 44, 93, 220 a, 220 b, 225, 239, 242, 247, 249

Yale University, Art Museum, Nos. 31 a, 35, 45, 56

Hanfstaengl, Munich, Nos. 54, 79, 88, 123

Gal. Silberman, Vienna, No. 202

NOTES

1. CATALAN SCHOOL, middle or second half of 12th century.

Christ as ruler of the world, with the symbols of the Evangelists on either side; beneath, Apostles and episodes from the Life of Christ. Mural painting from the apse of Santa Maria de Mur, Spain. Purchased 1920.

Boston, Massachusetts, Museum of Fine Arts.

Gertrud Richert, Mittelalterliche Malerei in Spanien, p. 12; C. R. Post, A History of Spanish Painting, I, p. 119.

2. MASTER OF THE ST. GEORGE, active in Catalonia in the early 15th century.

St. George and the Dragon. On wood ($55^1/_2 \times 37^3/_4$ inches). About 1430. Originally attributed to Benito Martorell and thought to be connected with the four panels of the St. George legend in the Louvre; Post assigns all these panels to an anonymous master.

Chicago, Illinois, Art Institute.

C. R. Post, A History of Spanish Painting, II, pp. 393 seq.

3. CATALAN SCHOOL, 15th century.

St. Martin of Tours with the beggar. On wood ($67^3/_4 \times 40^1/_8$).

Boston, Massachusetts, Museum of Fine Arts.

4. BARTOLOMÉ BERMEJO, active at Daroca, province of Saragossa; died after 1490.

St. Engracia. On wood ($64^1/_8 \times 28^3/_8$ inches). According to Hendy, painted about 1477. Purchased from the Somzée Collection in 1904.

Boston, Isabella Stewart Gardner Museum.

Philip Hendy, Catalogue of the Exhibited Paintings and Drawings, Boston 1931, pp. 40 seq.

5. EL GRECO (DOMENICO THEOTOCOPULI), born 1541 near Candia; died 1614 in Toledo. Assumption of the Virgin. On canvas ($151^1/_2 \times 77^1/_8$ inches). Signed and dated 1577. From San Domingo el Antiguo, Toledo.

Chicago, Illinois, Art Institute.

A. L. Mayer, El Greco, 1926, No. 114.

6. — St. Martin with the beggar. On canvas ($75^1/_4 \times 38^1/_2$ inches). Signed. Painted between December 1597 and the autumn of 1599 for the chapel of San José in Toledo, where the picture remained until 1906.

Elkins Park, Pennsylvania, Joseph Widener Collection.

A. L. Mayer, El Greco, 1926, No. 297.

7. — Madonna with the Child and Saints Agnes and Marina (or Tecla?). On canvas ($75^1/_4 \times 38^1/_2$ inches). Signed. Date and original location the same as its pendant, No. 6.

Elkins Park, Pennsylvania, Joseph Widener Collection.

A. L. Mayer, El Greco, 1926, No. 35.

8. — Fray Hortensio Felix Paravicini. On canvas ($43^1/_4 \times 33$ inches). Signed, 1609. Purchased in 1904 from the collection of the Duke of Arcos, Madrid.

Boston, Massachusetts, Museum of Fine Arts.

A. L. Mayer, El Greco, No. 335 a.

9. — Cardinal Don Fernando Nino de Guevara, Archbishop of Toledo (Cardinal from 1596; from 1601 Archbishop of Seville and Grand Inquisitor; died 1609). On canvas ($48 \times 42^1/_2$ inches). Signed. Painted between 1596 and 1600. From the Havemeyer collection.

New York, Metropolitan Museum.

A. L. Mayer, El Greco, 1926, No. 331.

10. — Toledo during a thunderstorm. On canvas ($47^5/_8 \times 41^3/_4$ inches). Signed. A late work. From the Havemeyer collection.

New York, Metropolitan Museum.

A. L. Mayer, El Greco, 1926, No. 315.

11. — Female portrait (formerly known as the Princess Eboli, or Greco's wife). On wood ($15^3/_4 \times 13$ inches). Painted, according to Mayer, 1578-81; according to Cossío, 1594 to 1604; according to E. K. Waterhouse, 1577.

Philadelphia, Pennsylvania, John G. Johnson Collection.

A. L. Mayer, El Greco, 1926, No. 351; Cossío, El Greco, 1908, No. 269.

12. DIEGO VELÁZQUEZ, born 1599 in Seville; died 1660 in Madrid.

Luis de Góngora (poet, 1561-1627). On canvas (20 × 16¹/₈ inches). Probably painted in the spring of 1622.

Boston, Massachusetts, Museum of Fine Arts.

*Klassiker der Kunst*⁴, *21*.

13. — Portrait of a Man. On canvas (20¹/₂ × 15³/₄ inches). An early work, about 1623. Purchased 1929.

Detroit, Michigan, Institute of Art.

A. L. Mayer, in Pantheon, IV, July 1929; Catalogue of Paintings in the Permanent Collection... 1930, No. 235.

14. — Don Balthasar Carlos and his Dwarf, the so-called child of Vallecas. On canvas (55 × 32 inches). Painted about 1631. From the collection of the Earl of Carlisle.

Boston, Massachusetts, Museum of Fine Arts.

*Klassiker der Kunst*⁴, *49*.

15. — King Philip IV of Spain. On canvas (53 × 35¹/₂ inches). Painted at Fraga in June 1644. There is a replica at Dulwich, which A. de Beruete identified as the work of Juan Bautista Martinez del Mazo. Purchased in 1911 from the estate of the Duke of Parma.

New York, Frick Art Museum.

*Klassiker der Kunst*⁴, *113*.

16. FRANCISCO DE ZURBARÁN, born 1598 at Fuente de Cantos, Badajoz; died 1664.

A Doctor of Salamanca University. On canvas (76 × 40¹/₂ inches). Purchased in 1910 from the Stchoukine collection.

Boston, Massachusetts, Isabella Stewart Gardner Museum.

Philip Hendy, Catalogue, Boston 1931, p. 428.

17. BARTOLOMÉ ESTEBAN MURILLO, born 1618 in Seville; died there, 1682.

Don Andrea de Andrade y Col (Master of Ceremonies of Seville Cathedral). On canvas (106¹/₄ × 46³/₄ inches). According to Mayer, painted between 1650 and 1660. Purchased in 1927 from the collection of the Earl of Northbrook.

New York, Metropolitan Museum.

Klassiker der Kunst, 222.

18. ZURBARÁN.

Return of the Holy Family from Egypt. On canvas (74¹/₂ × 96¹/₂ inches).

Toledo, Ohio, Museum of Art.

19. MURILLO.

St. Thomas of Villanueva as a Child, giving away his clothes to beggars. On canvas (86¹/₄ × 58¹/₄ inches). From the Amery collection.

Cincinnati, Ohio, Art Museum.

20. MURILLO.

Girl with her Duenna at a window ("Las Gallegas"). On canvas (49 × 41 inches).

Elkins Park, Pennsylvania, Joseph Widener Collection.

Klassiker der Kunst, 211.

21. FRANCISCO GOYA, born in 1746 at Fuendetodos, Aragon; died at Bordeaux in 1828.

Women on a balcony. On canvas (73³/₄ × 40 inches). Painted in 1810-15. From the Havemeyer collection.

New York, Metropolitan Museum.

A. L. Mayer, Goya, No. 627.

22. — Maria Luisa of Parma, wife of King Charles IV of Spain. On canvas (43¹/₄ × 32³/₄ inches). Painted in 1790-92. From the Havemeyer collection.

New York, Metropolitan Museum.

A. L. Mayer, Goya, No. 149.

23. — The Duchess of Alba. On canvas (82³/₄ × 58¹/₄ inches). Signed, 1797. Formerly in the Galerie Espagnole at the Louvre, Paris.

New York, The Hispanic Society of America.

Elisabeth Du Gué Trapier, Catalogue of Paintings, 16th, 17th and 18th Centuries, New York 1929, p. 243.

24. — Bullfight. On canvas (27¹/₂ × 36¹/₄ inches).

Toledo, Ohio, Museum of Art.

25. — Imaginary City on a rock. On canvas (31¹/₂ × 39³/₈ inches). Painted between 1815 and 1818. From the Havemeyer collection.

New York, Metropolitan Museum.

A. L. Mayer, Goya, No. 551.

26. — Fray Miguel Fernandez, Bishop of Marcopolis. On canvas (39³/₈ × 24³/₄ inches). Signed, 1815.

Worcester, Massachusetts, Art Museum.

A. L. Mayer, Goya, No. 258.

27. — Don Sebastian Martinez. On canvas (37 × 26³/₈ inches). Signed, 1792. Purchased 1906.

New York, Metropolitan Museum.

A. L. Mayer, Goya, No. 339.

28. — Gallants and a girl. On canvas (72¹/₂ × 39³/₄ inches). Reminiscent of Goya's tapestry cartoons, about 1779-80.

New York, Samuel H. Kress Collection.

A. L. Mayer, in Pantheon, I.

29. ITALIAN SCHOOL, showing Byzantine influence, last quarter of 13th century.

The Last Judgement. On wood (24¹/₂ × 24¹/₂ inches). The panel was assigned by Henniker-

Heaton to Umbria or Tuscany, by L. Venturi to Venice.

Worcester, Massachusetts, Art Museum.

Henniker-Heaton, in Art in America, February 1924; L. Venturi, Italian Paintings in America, No. 9.

30 a. DUCCIO DI BUONINSEGNA, 1255-1319, at Siena.

Calling of the Apostles Peter and Andrew. On wood (17 × 17¹/₄ inches). Together with No. 30b and two pictures now in the John D. Rockefeller collection, New York, belonged originally to Duccio's Maestà in Siena Cathedral, and was thus painted about 1308-11. From the Mackay collection, Roslyn, Long Island.

New York, Samuel H. Kress Collection.

Venturi, No. 18.

30 b. — The Temptation of Christ. On wood (17 × 17¹/₄ inches). See above, No. 30a. From the Benson collection.

New York, Frick Art Museum.

Venturi, No. 17.

31 a. BERNARDINO DADDI, known to have been active in Florence from 1312 to 1348.

Vision of St. Dominic. On wood (15 × 13¹/₂ inches). Together with several other panels now in Paris, Posen and Berlin, belonged to the predella of an altar-piece in Santa Maria Novella, Florence, painted in 1338. From the J. J. Jarves collection.

New Haven, Connecticut, Yale University.

Venturi, No. 45.

31 b. GIOVANNI BARONZIO DA RIMINI, active in Rimini, 1345-1362.

Adoration of the Magi. On wood (21³/₄ × 24 inches). Dated by van Marle (Das unbekannte Meisterwerk, I) about 1344-5; L. Venturi relates it to the Nativity in the church of Sant' Agostino at Rimini. From the Otto Kahn collection, New York.

New York, Mogmar Art Foundation.

Venturi, No. 115.

32. PIETRO LORENZETTI, active in Siena from 1330 to 1344.

Madonna enthroned with the Child. On wood (48³/₄ × 28¹/₄ inches).

Philadelphia, Pennsylvania, John G. Johnson Collection.

Venturi, No. 80.

33. GIOTTO DI BONDONE, born in 1266 or 1267 at Colle di Vespignano, near Florence; died in 1337 at Florence.

The Presentation in the Temple. On wood 17¹/₄ × 17 inches). The panel is related to five

others now in New York, Munich and the Berenson collection at Settignano, and was originally destined for a Franciscan church. That it is by Giotto's own hand has been doubted by Rintelen, Van Marle and Weigelt, but affirmed by Sirén, Hendy and L. Venturi. Purchased in 1900 from the J. P. Richter collection.

Boston, Massachusetts, Isabella Stewart Gardner Museum.

Venturi, No. 31.

34. PAOLO VENEZIANO, active in Venice from 1333 to 1358.

St. Maria Egyptiaca (11 × 7¹/₈ inches). Centre panel of a polyptych the arrangement of which was formerly different. On the back, St. Blasius. Has also been attributed to Lorenzo Veneziano.

Worcester, Massachusetts, Art Museum.

Venturi, No. 80.

35. SASSETTA, active in Siena 1392-1451.

St. Anthony assailed by demons. On wood (18¹/₄ × 13¹/₂ inches). Part of a polyptych, of which the other panels are now at Yale University, in the collections of P. Lehmann, D. F. Platt, at Englewood, and elsewhere. Purchased from the J. J. Jarves collection.

New Haven, Connecticut, Yale University.

Venturi, No. 141; Ellis K. Waterhouse in Burlington Magazine, 1931, 108.

36 a. — The Journey of the Three Magi. On wood (9 × 12 inches). Predella of a polyptych, of which the principal panel, the Nativity of the Virgin, is now in the Collegiata at Asciano. From the collection of the Marchioness of Crewe.

New York, Maitland Griggs Collection.

Venturi, No. 143.

36 b. GIOVANNI DI PAOLO, active in Siena, 1423-82.

Adam and Eve driven out of the Garden of Eden. On wood (18¹/₈ × 20¹/₂ inches). About 1450. From the Camille Benoit collection, Paris.

New York, P. Lehmann Collection.

Venturi, No. 161.

37. — John the Baptist in the Wilderness. On wood (25³/₄ × 15 inches). Related to five other panels now in Chicago, one in the P. Lehmann collection, New York, and two at Münster (Germany). From the Aynard collection, Lyons.

Chicago, Illinois, Art Institute.

Venturi, No. 165.

38. — Salome bringing the head of John Baptist on a charger. See preceding note.

Chicago, Illinois, Art Institute.

Venturi, No. 170.

39. STEFANO DA ZEVIO, born at Verona, 1375;
died at Trento, 1438.

The Virgin amidst rose-bushes. On wood
(24 × 17 inches).

Worcester, Massachusetts, Art Museum.

Venturi, No. 129.

40. MASOLINO, born at Panicale, 1383; died in
Rome, 1447.

Annunciation. On wood (58¼ × 45¼ inches).
Painted 1430-1440. From the collection of Lord
Wemyss, Gosford House, Longniddry, Had-
dingtonshire; Henry Goldman, New York.

Washington Museum.

Venturi, No. 188.

41. — Crucifixion. On wood (24½ × 19 inches).
Originally attributed to Giottino, and more
recently, by Berenson, to Rossello di Jacopo
Franchi; Venturi relates it to the frescoes in
Castiglione d'Olona and assigns it to Maso-
lino's early period.

New York, Maitland Griggs Collection.

Venturi, No. 185.

42. MASACCIO, born at San Giovanni Valdarno,
1401; died in Rome, 1429.

Young Man with turban. On wood (16¼ ×
11½ inches). According to Hendy, painted
between 1427 and 1429. Purchased in 1898.

Boston, Massachusetts, Isabella Stewart Gardner Museum.

Venturi, No. 192.

43. PAOLO UCCELLO, ca. 1397-1475, in Florence.

Portrait of a Young Lady. On wood (17¼ ×
12½ inches). Purchased in 1914 as a work of
Domenico Veneziano. Attributed by George
Pudelgo (Pantheon, March 1935) to one of
Uccello's pupils, the master of the Karlsruhe
Adoration. The Attribution to Uccello is con-
vincingly established by Hendy in his cata-
logue.

Boston, Massachusetts, Isabella Stewart Gardner Museum.

Venturi, No. 195.

44. FRANCESCO PESELLINO, active 1422-1477
in Florence.

Miracle of St. Sylvester. On wood (11½ ×
30½ inches). Originally formed a predella
together with two panels now in the Galleria
Doria, Rome. Generally considered to be an
early work, but assigned by Venturi to the
late period. Purchased in 1926.

Worcester, Massachusetts, Art Museum.

Venturi, No. 225.

45. ANTONIO POLLAIUOLO, born in Florence,
1429; died in Rome, 1498.

Rape of Dejanira. 1867. Transferred from
wood to canvas (21½ × 31¾ inches). Purchased by Jarves as a Pollaiuolo ("Once when
I discovered a beautiful Pollaiuolo, the owner
would not sell it to me except on the condi-
tion that I should buy all the 44 pictures in
the room as well."). At that time the figure
of Dejanira was completely overpainted, and
the centaur and landscape had been skilfully
developed, perhaps, according to Sirén, by the
artist himself as early as the time of Savona-
rola. According to the same writer the Nessus
and Dejanira are by a weaker hand than the
rest of the picture, perhaps Piero Pollaiuolo's.
From the J. J. Jarves collection.

New Haven, Connecticut, Yale University.

Venturi, No. 45.

46. PIERO POLLAIUOLO, born in Florence, 1443;
died in Rome, 1496.

Portrait of a Young Lady. On wood (18½ ×
11¾ inches). According to Hendy, the girl is
probably the model who sat for the St. Fina
in Piero's Coronation of the Virgin at San
Gimignano. Purchased in 1907 from the Oskar
Hainauer collection, Berlin.

Boston, Isabella Stewart Gardner Museum.

Venturi, No. 238.

47. ANDREA CASTAGNO, born at Castagno,
1423; died in Florence, 1457.

Bust-portrait of a young man. On wood
(20¾ × 15¼ inches). Probably painted between 1445 and 1450. Formerly attributed to
Botticelli, and by Berenson to A. Pollaiuolo.
From the Kann collection, Paris.

New York, Pierpont Morgan Library.

Venturi, No. 234.

48. — The Youthful David. Painted on a leather
shield (44⅞ × 31¾ inches at the top, by
17 inches at the bottom). Formerly attributed
to A. Pollaiuolo. From the Drury-Lowe collection, Locko Park.

Elkins Park, Pennsylvania, Joseph Widener
Collection.

Venturi, No. 235.

49. COSIMA TURA, about 1430-1495, in Ferrara.

Adoration of the Magi. On wood (15¼ ×
15⅛ inches). Belongs with the Circumcision in
the Gardner Museum, Boston, and the Flight
into Egypt from the former Benson collection,
London. Purchased in 1905 from the collection
of the Countess Santa Fiora, Rome.

Cambridge, Massachusetts, Fogg Art Museum.

Venturi, No. 346.

50. COLANTONIO, active in Naples about the
middle of the 15th century.

Male Portrait. On wood (23½ × 17¾ inches).
Formerly attributed to Ghirlandaio, and by

Berenson to Justus of Ghent; the attribution to Colantonio was established by Aru (Dedalo, 1931, p. 1121). From the Liberty E. Holden collection.

Cleveland, Ohio, Museum of Art.

Venturi, No. 374.

51. SANDRO BOTTICELLI, 1444-1510, in Florence.

Lorenzo Lorenzano. On wood (19¹/₄ × 14¹/₂ inches). The sitter was professor at the University of Pisa during the last quarter of the 15ᵗʰ century, and committed suicide in 1502. Painted about 1490. From the collection of Baron Lazzaroni, Paris.

Philadelphia, John G. Johnson Collection.

Venturi, No. 253.

52. — Communion of St. Jerome. On wood (13 × 9³/₄ inches). Painted in Florence, about 1490, for Francesco di Filippo del Pugliese, who mentions the picture in his will, dated February 28ᵗʰ 1502/3. From the Altman collection, Palazzo Capponi. Several replicas are known.

New York, Metropolitan Museum.

Venturi, No. 254.

53. — Madonna with an Angel, who hands grapes and ears of corn to the Child. On wood (33 × 24³/₄ inches). The angel's gifts symbolize the Eucharist. About 1470. From the Chigi collection in Rome. Purchased in 1899.

Boston, Isabella Stewart Gardner Museum.

Venturi, No. 243.

54. — Adoration of the Magi. On wood (28 × 41 inches). According to Horne (Botticelli, London, 1906), painted about 1482; according to Klassiker der Kunst (p. 20), originated in 1472-3. A recent purchase from the Hermitage, Leningrad.

Washington, D. C., Museum.

Klassiker der Kunst, 20.

55. FRANCESCO DI GIORGIO, 1439-1502, in Siena.

Young couple playing chess. On wood (13¹/₄ × 16 inches). The scene depicted, probably taken from a Novella, is as unintelligible as that of the pendant in the Loewenstein collection, Brussels.

New York, Maitland Griggs Collection.

Venturi, No. 305.

56. DOMENICO GHIRLANDAIO, 1449-94, in Florence.

Portrait of a lady. Fresco (20¹/₂ × 15 inches). Sirén thinks that the head resembles one of the portraits in the Visitation in Santa Maria Novella, Florence. From the J. J. Jarves collection.

New Haven, Connecticut, Yale University.

Sirén, Catalogue, 139 seq.

57. LORENZO DI CREDI, 1459/60-1537, in Florence.

Self-portrait. On wood (17 × 11¹/₂ inches). On the back, described as not by the artist's own hand, but nevertheless a self-portrait, painted in 1488. From the Beattie collection, Glasgow.

Elkins Park, Pennsylvania, Joseph Widener Collection.

Venturi, No. 281.

58. FRA BARTOLOMEO DELLA PORTA, 1472 to 1517, in Florence.

The Virgin and Child with Saints Mary Magdalen and John the Baptist. Perhaps painted with the assistence of Albertinelli. Purchased 1930.

New York, Metropolitan Museum.

59. LUCA SIGNORELLI, about 1450-1523, in Cortona.

Virgin and Child. On wood (20¹/₄ × 18¹/₂ inches). A late work. From the Benson collection, London.

New York, Jules S. Bache Collection.

Venturi, No. 278.

60. FILIPPINO LIPPI, ca. 1457-1504, in Florence.

Adoration of the Child. On wood (32 × 28³/₄ inches). Assigned by Venturi to Lippi's middle period; attributed by Scharf to Raffaelino del Garbo. From the Dreyfus collection, Paris.

Toledo, Ohio, Museum of Art.

Venturi, No. 262.

61. — The Holy Family with Saints John and Margaret. On wood, round (diameter 61¹/₄ inches). According to Scharf (Filippino Lippi, Vienna, 1935), painted in 1497; in any case a late work. There is a copy at Zagreb. Purchased in 1929 from the L. E. Holden collection.

Cleveland, Ohio, Museum of Art.

Venturi, No. 264.

62. BARTOLOMEO VIVARINI, active in Venice from 1450 to 1499.

Virgin and Child. On wood (32³/₄ × 25³/₄ inches). Signed, 1472.

New York, Metropolitan Museum.

Venturi, No. 356.

63. ANDREA MANTEGNA, born at Vicenza, 1431; died at Mantua, 1506.

St. Jerome. On wood (30 × 21¹/₂ inches). Reproduced by L. Venturi, 1927, as an early work of Mantegna, and dated by him before the Eremitani frescoes. From the Otto Kahn collection.

Washington, D. C., Museum.

Venturi, No. 338.

64. — Tarquin and the Sibyl (perhaps Catherine before the Sultan? cf. the painting by the Bruges master, about 1460, in the John G. Johnson Collection, Philadelphia, Cat. II, 319). On canvas (22³/₄ × 19 inches). According to L. Venturi, painted at the end of the 15ᵗʰ century; according to Berenson, a late work; according to A. Venturi and Kristeller, a workshop production. From the collection of the Duke of Buccleuch, Montague House, London; then Mrs. M. Emery.

Cincinnati, Ohio, Art Museum.

Venturi, No. 341.

65. — Judith. On wood (12 × 7 inches). With the Parnassus, to be dated about 1490. From the collections of Lorenzo de' Medici, Charles I of England, and the Earl of Pembroke. Purchased in 1917.

Elkins Park, Pennsylvania, Joseph Widener Collection.

Venturi, No. 340; see also Schwabe, in Burlington Magazine XXXIII, where the relationship to other versions of the subject is discussed.

66. ANTONELLO DA MESSINA, active at Messina from 1457 to 1479.

Head of a youth. On wood (10¹/₂ × 8 inches). Closely related to the head of a youth in the Johnson Collection, Philadelphia. From the B. Altman collection.

New York, Metropolitan Museum.

Venturi, No. 379.

67. GIOVANNI BELLINI, active 1459-1516 in Venice.

Portrait of a youth. On wood (11 × 9 inches). Formerly described as Venetian School about 1505, but ascribed by Berenson to Giovanni Bellini, and more recently by L. Venturi to Boccaccino. From the collection of Sir Charles Robinson, London.

Elkins Park, Pennsylvania, Joseph Widener Collection.

Venturi, No. 426.

68. JACOPO DA VALENCIA, active 1485-1509 in Venice.

St. Jerome. On wood (23¹/₂ × 16³/₄ inches). Purchased in 1926.

Boston, Massachusetts, Museum of Fine Arts.

69. CARLO CRIVELLI, active 1457-93 in Venice and the Marches.

Pietà. On wood (34¹/₂ × 20³/₄ inches). Signature and date 1485 by a later hand, probably an imitation of the original hand. From the Panciaticchi collection, Florence.

Boston, Massachusetts, Museum of Fine Arts.

Venturi, No. 370.

70. GENTILE BELLINI, active 1460-1507 in Venice.

A Turkish painter. Pen and wash on parchment, copied at the beginning of the 16ᵗʰ century by the Persian miniaturist Behzad. (7¹/₈ × 5¹/₂ inches). Painted an 1479-80 and purchased in 1907.

Boston, Massachusetts, Isabella Stewart Gardner Museum.

Martin, in Burlington Magazine, IX, 1906, pp. 148 seq.

71. JACOPO DE BARBARI, about 1450-1516 (?), in Venice.

Lovers of unequal age. On wood (15³/₄ × 12³/₄ inches). Signed, 1503. From the Weber collection, Hamburg.

Philadelphia, Pennsylvania, John G. Johnson Collection.

Venturi, No. 420.

72. GIOVANNI BELLINI, see No. 67.

St. Francis in landscape. On wood (48³/₄ × 54 inches). Signed. Painted about 1480. According to Antonio Michiel, at the beginning of the 16ᵗʰ century this painting was in the Palazzo Contarini, Venice.

New York, Frick, Art Museum.

Venturi, No. 390.

73. — Bacchanal. On canvas (66 × 72³/₄ inches). Painted for the studio of Duke Alfonso of Ferrara, and dated by the artist 1514; according to Vasari it was finished by Titian. It is supposed that the landscape background was added by Titian. Passed from the collections of Cardinal Pietro Aldobrandini and Cardinal Lodovico Ludovisi in Rome to that of the Duke of Northumberland at Alnwick Castle.

Elkins Park, Pennsylvania, Joseph Widener Collection.

Venturi, No. 406.

74. VITTORE CARPACCIO, born about 1455 in Istria; died 1523 in Venice.

Meditation on the Passion of Christ. On wood (27³/₄ × 34 inches). With spurious signature of Andrea Mantegna. Painted about 1510. Closely related to the Entombment in Berlin, which likewise bears a spurious Mantegna signature. First reproduced and attributed to Carpaccio by Claude Phillips (Burlington Magazine 1911, p. 144). Purchased in 1911 from the collection of Sir William Neville Abdy, London.

New York, Metropolitan Museum.

Venturi, No. 408.

75. CIMA DA CONEGLIANO, 1459/60-1515/18 in Venice and in Friuli.

Silenus. On wood (11³/₄ × 16 inches). About 1500. Related to the Bacchus in the Poldi-Pezzoli collection, Milan. From the Adolf Thiem collection, San Remo.

Philadelphia, Pennsylvania, John G. Johnson Collection.

Venturi, No. 470.

76 a. RAPHAEL, born 1483 at Urbino; died 1520 in Rome.

Mourning for Christ. On wood (9 × 11 inches). Part of the predella of the Colonna altarpiece (see below), the other parts being now in the National Gallery, London (Christ bearing the Cross), in the Metropolitan Museum, New York (Christ on the Mount of Olives; see below, No. 76 b), at Dulwich (St. Anthony and a Franciscan Saint), and at Dresden (St. Francis). The predella passed from the collections of Christina of Sweden and Don Livio Odescalchi to the Duke of Orleans, and was broken up in the time of the latter's great-grandson, Philippe Égalité. On the further history of the Pietà until its purchase in 1900, see Hendy (Catalogue, p. 283).

Boston, Massachusetts, Isabella Stewart Gardner Museum.

Venturi, No. 443.

76 b. — Christ on the Mount of Olives. On wood (9¹/₂ × 11 inches). See above, No. 76 a. Some scholars consider this panel to be the work of a pupil, and the advanced composition, especially the Apostle on the right, does in fact point to a date later than 1505. Purchased in 1934 from the Clarence H. Mackay collection.

New York, Metropolitan Museum.

Venturi, No. 442.

77. — Madonna with Saints (the Colonna altarpiece). On wood (68¹/₈ × 67⁷/₈ inches; the lunette, 30 × 72 inches). Painted in 1504-5 for the convent of Sant' Antonio at Perugia. From 1677 to 1802 in the possession of the Colonna family, then in the collection of the King of the Two Sicilies, Francisco I. Purchased by Pierpont Morgan in 1901 and presented to the museum in 1916. On the predella, see above, No. 76.

New York, Metropolitan Museum.

Venturi, No. 441.

78. — The small Cowper Madonna. On wood (24 × 17 inches). Painted about 1505, and closely related to the Madonna del Granduca. From the collection of Lord Cowper, Panshanger.

Elkins Park, Pennsylvania, Joseph Widener Collection.

Venturi, No. 444.

79. — The Alba Madonna. Transferred from wood to canvas; round, diameter 37¹/₂ inches. Painted about 1508. During the 18th century

belonged to the Dukes of Alba, Madrid. Later at the Hermitage, Leningrad, whence it was recently purchased.

Washington, Museum.

Klassiker der Kunst⁴, 74.

80. — Count Tommaso Inghirami. On wood (35 × 24¹/₂ inches). The sitter (1470-1516) was a humanist and poet, and an important personage at the Papal Court. The portrait must have been painted about 1512-14, and until its purchase in 1898 remained in the Palazzo Inghirami at Volterra. A copy in the Palazzo Pitti, Florence, formerly supposed to be the original, is now held by most authorities to be a replica by Raphael himself or by another hand.

Boston, Massachusetts, Isabella Stewart Gardner Museum.

Hendy, Catalogue, p. 284.

81. TITIAN, born 1477 at Pieve di Cadore; died 1576, in Venice.

Portrait of a man. On canvas (30 × 25 inches). Previously attributed to Licinio, Sebastiano del Piombo, Giorgione, or held to be a copy after Giorgione, but claimed by Valentiner, Suida, L. Venturi and Tietze for Titian's early period and dated by them about 1510. From the Henry Doetsch collection, London and the Henry Goldman Collection, New York.

New York, Samuel H. Kress Collection.

Venturi, No. 505.

82. GIORGIONE, born about 1476 at Castelfranco; died 1510, in Venice.

The adoration of the Shepherds. On wood (35 × 42 inches). The picture is sometimes identified with one mentioned in the Catalogue of Pictures having belonged to king James the Second (No. 182). It can, however, only be traced with certainty back to the Collection of Cardinal Fesch in 1845; it passed later through the Collection of Claudius Tarrel, Beaumont and Allendale, London.

83. TITIAN.

Venus with the Flute Player. On canvas (62¹/₂ × 82 inches). This conception of a theme which has been passed down in several versions, was according to Hadeln (Pantheon 1932, p. 237 t) begun in the forties and finished about 1560, according to G. M. Richter (Burl. Mag. L. IX, p. 58) painted about 1560. The later dating of the whole work is most probable, owing to its manneristic features. From the Collection of the Earl of Leicester, Holkham Hall; New York, Metropolitan Museum.

Titian, Venus with the Flute Player, About 1560, New York, Metro Mus.

Tietze, Titian, 183; Wehle, Titian's Venus from Holkham, Metro. Mus. XXXI, 1936, 182.

84. BARTOLOMEO VENETO, active in Lombardy from 1502 to 1530.

Portrait of a young man (30³/₄ × 23¹/₄ inches). The sitter has been (not very convincingly) identified as Charles d'Amboise or Massimiliano Sforza. That the horseman an lansquenet in the background were borrowed from Dürer's woodcut B. 133, has often been noticed. From the Crespi collection, Milan and the Henry Goldman Collection, New York.

New York, Samuel H. Kress Collection.

Venturi, No. 476.

85. JACOPO PALMA IL VECCHIO, born about 1480 at Serina; died 1528 in Venice.

Portrait of a bearded man. On canvas (27¹/₄ × 21³/₄ inches).

Philadelphia, Pennsylvania, John G. Johnson Collection.

Venturi, No. 495.

86. SEBASTIANO DEL PIOMBO, born about 1495 in Venice; died 1547 in Rome.

Posthumous portrait of Christopher Columbus (1446—1506). On canvas (42¹/₄ × 33³/₄ inches). Signature and a long inscription dated 1519 (not by the artist's own hand). From the collections of the Duc de Talleyrand, Valencay, Sagan and J. P. Morgan. Purchased in 1900.

New York, Metropolitan Museum.

Venturi, No. 503.

87. TITIAN.

Man with a falcon. On canvas (43 × 37¹/₄ inches). The sitter has been identified, without reason, as Giorgio Cornaro or Federigo Gonzaga, and by L. Venturi as a member of the Este family, the same who is found in the Venus with the mirror formerly in the Goldman Collection, New York. This identification is a unconvincing as the previous ones. Painted about 1530. From the collection of the Earl of Carlisle, Castle Howard.

New York, Erickson Collection.

Venturi, No. 513.

88. — The Toilet of Venus. On canvas (48³/₄ × 41¹/₄ inches). In Titian's possession at his death. Painted about 1565. Several replicas exist. Purchased from the Hermitage, Leningrad.

Washington, D. C., Museum.

Klassiker der Kunst⁵, p. 178.

89. — Rape of Europa. On canvas (70 × 80³/₄ inches). Belongs to the series of mythological compositions painted by Titian for Philip II of Spain. First mentioned in a letter from Titian to the King dated June 19th, 1559, and described as having been dispatched in 1562. Passed through a number of celebrated collec-

tions to that of the Earl of Darnley at Cobham Hall, from which it was purchased in 1896.

Boston, Massachusetts, Isabella Stewart Gardner Museum.

Venturi, No. 527.

90. — Nicolas Perrenot Granvella. On canvas (44 × 34 inches). Signed. Probably painted at Augsburg in the autumn of 1548. From the R. A. Tattorn collection.

Kansas City, Missouri, William Rockhill Nelson Gallery of Art.

Venturi, No. 521.

91. LORENZO LOTTO, born about 1480 in Venice; died 1556, at Loreto.

St. Peter Martyr. On canvas (34³/₄ × 26³/₄ inches). Supposed to be referred to in an entry in Lotto's account-book in 1549, where mention is made of a St. Peter Martyr painted for Fra Angelo Ferretti of San Domenico, the picture having his measurements and being a portrait of him. From the Murray collection.

Cambridge, Massachusetts, Fogg Art Museum.

Venturi, No. 531.

92. GIOVANNI BATTISTA MORONI, born about 1525 at Bondo, near Bergamo; died 1578, at Bergamo.

Portrait of a Scholar. On canvas (38 × 29¹/₂ inches). The sitter was formerly described as "Titian's schoolmaster". The picture, noted by Van Dyck in his Chatsworth sketch-book, was in the Borghese collection, Rome, during the 18th century, and then passed to that of the Duke of Sutherland at Stafford House.

Elkins Park, Pennsylvania, Joseph Widener Collection.

Venturi, No. 543.

93. — The Captain of Bergamo. On canvas (34 × 24 inches). Painted shortly after 1560.

Worcester, Massachusetts, Art Museum.

Venturi, No. 541.

94. — Portrait of a priest. On canvas (23³/₄ × 28¹/₂ inches). Purchased in 1916 from the Abdy collection, London.

Minneapolis, Minnesota, Institute of Arts.

95. —The Prioress Lucrezia Cattaneo. On canvas (35³/₄ × 26¹/₂ inches). According to the inscription, painted in 1557.

New York, Metropolitan Museum.

Venturi, No. 537.

96. — Madonna with praying donor. On canvas (24 × 26 inches). The Madonna is imitated from Dürer's woodcut B. 32 (1516).

New York, Samuel H. Kress Collection.

97. GIOVANNI GIROLAMO SAVOLDO, born about 1480 at Brescia; died about 1550, in Venice.

St. Matthew and the Angel. On canvas (36³/₄ × 49¹/₄ inches). A late work.

New York, Metropolitan Museum.

Adolfo Venturi, Storia dell'Arte Italiana, IX, iii, p. 783.

98. JACOPO ROBUSTI, called TINTORETTO, 1518-94, in Venice.

St. Peter walking on the sea. On canvas (41 × 45 inches). Held by E. von der Bercken and A. L. Mayer (J. Tintoretto, Munich 1923) to be the master's earliest work (wrongly described as the Calling of Peter).

New York, G. L. Winthrop Collection.

99. — Baptism of Christ. On canvas (76¹/₂ × 100 inches). Dated by L. Venturi 1562-68.

New York, Arthur Sachs Collection, on loan to the Fogg Art Museum, Cambridge, Massachusetts.

100. PARIS BORDONE, born 1500 at Treviso; died 1570, in Venice.

Adoration of the Magi. On canvas (34¹/₄ × 39³/₄ inches). Signed. Painted about 1550-60. Formerly in the collection of the Archduke Leopold Wilhelm, being mentioned in the 1659 inventory; can be recognized in the painting of the Archduke's gallery by Teniers, in Brussels.

New York, G. L. Winthrop Collection.

E. Fröhlich-Bum, in Burlington Magazine, 1934, p. 282.

101. MICHELANGELO MERISI DA CARAVAGGIO, born 1570 at Caravaggio; died 1610 at Porto Ercole.

Card-players. (37³/₄ × 45³/₄ inches.) The attribution to Hendrik Ter Brugghen is rejected by Venturi, after a comparison with the picture of card-players in the Sciarra collection, Rome. Venturi dates it shortly before 1600.

Cambridge, Massachusetts, Fogg Art Museum.

Venturi, No. 580.

102. TINTORETTO, see above, No. 98.

Lady in black. Oil on canvas (45¹/₄ × 37³/₄ inches). Purchased in 1903 from Palazzo Chigi, Rome.

Boston, Massachusetts, Isabella Stewart Gardner Museum.

Hendy, Catalogue, p. 364.

103. BERNARDINO LUINI, ative 1512-32, in Milan.
Portrait of a Lady. On wood (29 × 21¹/₂ inches). From the Benson collection.

Washington, D. C., Museum.

Venturi, No. 488.

104. PAOLO VERONESE, born 1528 at Verona; died 1588, in Venice.

Portrait of a lady with her daughter. On canvas (81 × 47¹/₂ inches). The pendant, belonging to Conte Contini, Rome, is traditionally supposed to represent Conte Giuseppe Porto of Vicenza.

Baltimore, Maryland, Walters Art Gallery.

105. — Mars and Venus. On canvas (81 × 63³/₄ inches). Signed. Painted between 1576 and 1584 for the Emperor Rudolph II; afterwards belonged to Queen Christina of Sweden and various other collections; there is a replica in the Hermitage, Leningrad. Purchased in 1910.

New York, Metropolitan Museum.

Venturi, No. 571.

106. GORREGGIO, 1494-1534, in Modena.

Four Saints. On canvas (67³/₄ × 49¹/₂ inches). Painted about 1515 for the hospital of Santa Maria della Misericordia, Parma. For a long time in the possession of the Ashburton family, and known as the Ashburton altar-piece. Assigned by Morelli to its place in Correggio's work. Purchased in 1912.

New York, Metropolitan Museum.

Venturi, No. 469.

107. DOSSO DOSSI, born 1479 at Mantua; died 1542 at Modena.

The Three Ages of Man. On canvas (11 × 44¹/₄ inches). Formerly in the O. Sirén collection. Purchased in 1926.

New York, Metropolitan Museum.

A. Venturi, Storia dell'Arte Italiana, IX, iii, p. 967.

108. DOMENICO BECCAFUMI, 1486-1551, in Siena.

Portrait of a Gentleman. On wood (34³/₄ × 23¹/₄ inches). Previously assigned to Lotto, Cavazzola, and Sebastiano del Piombo, but Venturi's attribution to Beccafumi seems probable.

St. Louis, Missouri, City Art Museum.

Venturi, No. 466.

109. RIDOLFO GHIRLANDAIO, 1483-1561, in Florence.

Florentine Nobleman. On wood (25 × 19 inches). First identified by Bode; assigned by Gamba (Dedalo, IX, p. 465) to the early period. Formerly in the Brancacci collection, Rome; then Martin A. Ryerson, Chicago.

Chicago, Illinois, Art Institute.

Venturi, No. 448.

110. JACOPO CARRUCCI called PONTORMO, born 1494 at Pontormo, near Empoli; died 1556-7 in Florence.

The Halberdier. On canvas ($37^1/_2 \times 29$ inches). Painted about 1528-30. The identification proposed by Voss (Malerei der Spätrenaissance, 1921, p. 171) with a portrait of Francesco Guardi mentioned by Vasari, has been rejected by Wehle and F. J. Mather (Art in America, 1922, p. 66). Formerly in the collections of Cardinal Fesch, Princess Mathilde Bonaparte, and C. C. Stillman, New York.

New York, Metropolitan Museum.

Venturi, No. 458.

111. BACCIO BANDINELLI, 1488(?)-1559, in Florence.

Self-portrait. On wood (58×44 inches); addition by another hand along lower edge. The Order of Santiago and the drawing of Hercules and Bacchus enable us to date the picture after 1530. When purchased in 1899 from the Vivian collection was thought to be a Portrait of Michelangelo by Sebastiano del Piombo; the names of Salviati and Rosso have also been proposed.

Boston, Massachusetts, Isabella Stewart Gardner Museum.

Venturi, No. 461.

112. BERNARDO STROZZI, born 1581 in Genoa; died 1644 in Venice.

St. Catherine. On canvas ($67^3/_4 \times 47^1/_4$ inches). Purchased in 1931 from the Sumner collection.

Hartford, Connecticut, Wadsworth Atheneum.

Venturi, No. 581.

113. GIAMBATTISTA TIEPOLO, born 1696 in Venice; died 1770 in Spain.

Portrait of a Lady. On canvas. Venturi dates the picture from the sitter's Spanish costume between 1762 and 1770.

Cleveland, Ohio, Henry G. Dalton Collection.

Venturi, No. 595.

114. GIOVANNI BATTISTA PIAZZETTA, 1682 to 1754, in Venice.

Joseph sold into bondage by his brethren. On canvas (44×67 inches). Purchased in 1922. The picture has been given to Domenico Maggiotto (1713-93) by Rodolfo Pallucchini in Rivista di Venezia, 1932, p. 492.

New York, Metropolitan Museum.

115. GIAMBATTISTA TIEPOLO.

Rinaldo bewitched by Armida. On canvas ($74^3/_4 \times 101^1/_2$ inches). One of a series of four pictures illustrating Tasso's "Gerusalemme Liberata". Venturi dates the series, of which several versions exist, 1737-51. Etchings of the series were made by Domenico Tiepolo. Formerly in the Serbelloni collection, Venice, and that of James Deering, Chicago.

Chicago, Illinois, Art Institute.

Venturi, No. 589.

116. ALESSANDRO MAGNASCO, 1681-1747, in Genoa.

The Synagogue. On canvas ($47^1/_4 \times 58^3/_4$ inches). The latest version of a subject which the artist often treated and of which two other versions have been preserved.

Cleveland, Ohio, Museum of Art.

Venturi, No. 583.

117. GIOVANNI PAOLO PANNINI, born 1691 or 1695 at Piacenza; died 1768 in Rome.

Sketch for the picture of Piazza Navona in the museum at Dublin. On canvas ($10^5/_8 \times 14^3/_4$ inches).

Chicago, Illinois, Art Institute.

118 a. PIETRO LONGHI, 1702-83, in Venice.

The pretended fainting-fit. On canvas ($19^1/_4 \times 24$ inches). From the collection of Prince Giovanelli, Venice.

New York, Samuel H. Kress Collection.

Venturi, No. 600.

118 b. — Blind-man's-buff. As the preceding picture.

New York, Samuel H. Kress Collection.

119 a. FRANCESCO GUARDI, 1712-93, in Venice.

Festival on the Grand Canal. On canvas ($39^3/_4 \times 65^3/_4$ inches).

Philadelphia, Pennsylvania, John G. Johnson Collection.

Venturi, No. 612.

119 b. — The Rialto. On canvas ($26^3/_4 \times 35^1/_2$ inches). From the Ingram collection, Marsala.

Elkins Park, Pennsylvania, Joseph Widener Collection.

Venturi, No. 609.

120. JAN VAN EYCK, born about 1380 to 1390 at Maaseyck on the Maas; died 1441 at Bruges.

St. Francis receiving the Stigmata. On wood ($4^7/_8 \times 6^1/_8$ inches). Painted about 1438. Purchased from the collection of Lord Heytesbury in 1890. Another version, identical in composition but twice as large, is in the Turin gallery. Whereas Kämmerer, Voll and Dvorak consider this version to be a later copy and Phillips denies its authenticity, Weale, Waagen, Bock, Bodenhausen, Jaccacci, Valentiner and Friedländer maintain that this is the original version.

Philadelphia, Pennsylvania, John G. Johnson Collection.

Friedländer, Altniederländische Malerei, I, p. 101, plate XLVI; Catalogue, II, 314.

121. PETRUS CHRISTUS, born about 1415 at Baerle, near Tilborg; died about 1473 at Bruges.

St. Eligius. On wood ($38^1/_2 \times 33^1/_2$ inches). Formerly supposed to represent St. Godeberta, whom St. Eligius is betrothing to Christ in the presence of King Lothair. Later explained as portrait of an engaged couple with Eligius. According to Friedländer the personages lack the characteristics of portraiture, so that he believes it to represent an imaginary engaged couple with St. Eligius. Purchased in 1914 from the A. Oppenheim collection, Cologne.

New York, P. Lehmann Collection.

Friedländer, I, p. 146.

122. — Annunciation. On wood ($30^3/_4 \times 25^3/_4$ inches). According to Friedländer closely related to the works of Jan van Eyck, but preferably to be attributed to Hubert van Eyck, as was asserted verbally by Panofsky. Purchased in 1932 from the M. Friedsam collection.

New York, Metropolitan Museum.

123. JAN VAN EYCK, see above, No. 120.

Annunciation. Transferred from wood to canvas ($36^1/_4 \times 15$ inches). Evidently the left wing of a triptych. Painted about 1434. Purchased in 1934 from the Hermitage, Leningrad.

Washington, D. C., Museum.

Friedländer, I, p. 104.

124. PETRUS CHRISTUS.

Portrait of a Carthusian Monk. On wood ($8^1/_2 \times 11^5/_8$ inches). Signed, 1466. From the Dos Aguas collection, Valencia. According to Friedländer, the halo must have been added later. The sitter is sometimes identified as the Carthusian Dionysius of Louvain, 1402-71, who had a reputation for saintliness.

New York, Jules S. Bache Collection.

Friedländer, I, p. 145.

125. ROGIER VAN DER WEYDEN, born about 1400 at Tournai; died 1464 in Brussels.

St. Luke painting the Virgin. On wood ($54^1/_4 \times 53^1/_2$ inches). Purchased in 1893. Of this composition four outher versions are known, of which the one in Munich was formerly supposed to be the original; this, however, was disputed by Hulin (Catalogue Critique, p. 28); since the Boston version was cleaned in 1933, it has generally been held to be the original, but this in turn has recently been disputed by Leo van Puyvelde (Burlington Magazine, August 1935).

Boston, Massachusetts, Museum of Fine Arts.

Friedländer, II, No. 106c; P. Hendy, A Rogier v. d. Weyden Altar-piece, in Burlington Magazine, 1933, pp. 33 seq.

126. — Meliaduse d'Este. On wood ($15 \times 9^3/_4$ inches). On the back arms of the Este family with initials and device (repr. Burl. Mag., XVIII, p. 202). Probably painted in 1450, as

the hammer in the sitter's hand must refer to the opening of the Porta Santa. Purchased in 1932 from the Friedsam collection.

New York, Metropolitan Museum.

Friedländer, II, No. 23, as Lionello d'Este; Catalogo della Esposizione della Pittura Ferrarese del Rinascimento, 1933.

127. — Portrait of a young woman. On wood ($14^3/_8 \times 10^5/_8$ inches). Painted about 1455. From the ducal castle at Dessau.

Washington, D. C., Museum.

Friedländer, II, No. 29a.

128. DIRK BOUTS, born about 1410 at Haarlem; died 1475 at Louvain.

Portrait of a man in a cap. On wood ($11^1/_4 \times 8^1/_4$ inches). From the A. Oppenheim collection, Cologne, and that of B. Altman, New York. Purchased in 1913.

New York, Metropolitan Museum.

Friedländer, III, No. 32.

129. — Moses and the Burning Bush. On wood ($17^1/_8 \times 13^1/_2$ inches). From the Kann collection, Paris.

Philadelphia, Pennsylvania, John G. Johnson Collection.

Friedländer, III, No. 13.

130. HUGO VAN DER GOES, born about 1440 at Ghent; died 1482 at Roodenclooster, near Brussels.

Portrait of a praying man. On wood ($12^5/_8 \times 10^1/_2$ inches). Rounded off to Form an oval. Formerly attributed to Antonello da Messina, and by Puyvelde (Burlington Magazine, August 1935) to Mabuse. Purchased in 1922 from the collection of Mrs. Havemeyer.

New York, Metropolitan Museum.

131. — Portrait of a Donor with John the Baptist. On wood ($13^1/_8 \times 9$ inches). Probably a fragment. A late work. Purchased in 1920 from the Leembruggen collection.

Baltimore, Maryland, Walters Art Gallery.

Friedländer, IV, No. 18.

132a. HANS MEMLING, born about 1430, possibly at Memelynck, near Alkmaar; died 1494, at Bruges.

Thomas Portinari. On wood ($17^1/_4 \times 13^1/_4$ inches). Generally dated about 1472, as both Portinari and his wife, on the pendant to this picture, appear rather younger than on the altar-piece executed in 1474 at Florence. Purchased in 1913 from the B. Altman collection.

New York, Metropolitan Museum.

Friedländer, VI, No. 69.

132 b. — Madonna and Child. On wood ($13^3/_4 \times$ $10^1/_4$ inches). Friedländer dates the picture about 1485. Formerly in a Spanish collection, afterwards in that of Martin A. Ryerson.

Chicago, Illinois, Art Institute.

Friedländer, VI, No. 50.

133. JUSTUS OF GHENT, active about 1460-80; at first in Ghent; after 1468, in Italy.

Adoration of the Magi. Water-colours on canvas ($39^3/_8 \times 62^1/_4$ inches). Probably painted in 1466, in any case in Ghent, before 1468, when Justus went to Italy. From a Spanish collection.

New York, George Blumenthal Collection.

Friedländer, III, 101 D; see also L. Demont, in Revue d'Art, XXV, 56.

134. MASTER OF THE VIRGO INTER VIRGINES, active in last quarter of 15th century at Delft or Gouda.

Mourning for the Dead Christ. On wood ($34^1/_2 \times 20$ inches). Friedländer places it in the periphery of the anonymous master's work as he has reconstructed it. Purchased in 1926 from the collection of Dr. U. Thieme, Leipzig.

New York, Metropolitan Museum.

Friedländer, V, No. 59.

135. HANS MEMLING, s. above No. 132 a.

The Virgin with the Child and two Angels. On wood ($22 \times 19^1/_4$ inches). Painted about 1480 as a further development of the Granada Madonna and as a preliminary to the Madonna in Florence (Friedländer). From the Gothic House in Wörlitz, near Dessau.

Washington, D. C., Museum.

Friedländer, VI, No. 60.

136. MASTER OF THE ST. LUCY LEGEND, active in last quarter of t5th century at Bruges.

The Virgin with female Saints in a rose-garden. On wood ($30^3/_4 \times 23^5/_8$ inches). On account of its similarity to the 1489 Madonna in Brussels, Valentiner dates this picture from the same period. Purchased in 1926 from the Weber collection, Brussels.

Detroit, Institute of Art.

Friedländer, VI, No. 68; Catalogue of Paintings (Valentiner), 1930, No. 140.

137. GERARD DAVID, born about 1460 at Oudewater; died 1523 at Bruges.

Mourning for Christ beneath the Cross. On wood ($33 \times 24^1/_2$ inches). The wings belonging to this picture are in the P. Lehmann collection, New York. Friedländer dates it before 1511.

Philadelphia, Pennsylvania, John G. Johnson Collection.

Friedländer, VI, No. 163.

138. HIERONYMUS BOSCH, born about 1462 at Hertogenbosch; died there 1516.

The Mocking of Christ. On wood ($19^3/_4 \times 20^1/_2$ inches). From the W. B. Paterson collection, London.

Philadelphia, Pennsylvania, John G. Johnson Collection.

Friedländer, V, No. 78.

139. — Adoration of the Magi. On wood ($28^1/_4 \times$ 22 inches). An early work, closely related to the Adoration of the Magi in the Prado, Madrid. Purchased in 1912 from the Lippmann collection, Berlin.

New York, Metropolitan Museum.

Friedländer, V, No. 66.

140. QUENTIN MASSYS, born 1460 or 1466 at Louvain; died 1530 at Antwerp.

Bust-portrait of a woman, in an architectural framework. On wood ($19^1/_4 \times 16^3/_4$ inches). Purchased in 1932 from the Friedsam collection.

New York, Metropolitan Museum.

Friedländer, VII, No. 48.

141. — Man with a pink. On wood ($17^1/_2 \times 11^1/_2$ inches). From the collection of Prince P. Demidoff.

Chicago, Illinois, Art Institute.

Friedländer, VIII, No. 47.

142 a. — St. Mary Magdalen. On wood ($11^1/_2 \times$ $7^7/_8$ inches). Purchased in 1909 from the collection of Count Nesselrode, Amsterdam.

Philadelphia, Pennsylvania, John G. Johnson Collection.

Friedländer, VII, No. 7.

142 b. — St. Mary Egyptiaca. Pendant to the preceding picture.

Philadelphia, Pennsylvania, John G. Johnson Collection.

Friedländer, VII, No. 7.

143. JOACHIM PATINIR, born 1485 at Dinant; died 1525 at Antwerp.

Rest on the Flight into Egypt. On wood ($13^3/_8 \times 19^1/_4$ inches). The figures are attributed to Massys, whereas in a picture of the same subject in the Johnson Collection, Philadelphia, both figures and landscape, according to Valentiner, are the work of Patinir. The episode depicted is the legend according to which the Holy Family, on their flight into Egypt, were closely pursued by Herod's soldiers and were saved by the miraculous growth of a wheatfield. The peasant was told to inform the pursuers that the fugitives had passed when he was sowing the wheat, but the Child Christ caused the wheat to grow up overnight, so that the soldiers gave up the pursuit, thinking that the fugitives were already beyond their reach.

Minneapolis, Minnesota, Institute of Arts.

Handbook of Paintings, 1926, p. 6.

144. — Assumption of the Virgin. On wood (22³/₄ × 22 inches). On the right coat of arms of Lukas Rehm of Augsburg, who, as representative of the Fuggers, lived in Antwerp until 1519-20, and whose arms occur on a winged altar-piece in Munich, formerly attributed to Patinir, and now assigned to Massys (M. J. Friedländer, Van Eyck bis Brueghel, 1916, p. 96). From the Charles Y. Yerkes collection, New York.

Philadelphia, Pennsylvania, John G. Johnson Collection.

Valentiner, in Catalogue, II, p. 378 and III, p. 214.

145. BERNARD VAN ORLEY, born 1491 or 1493 in Brussels; died there, 1541.

The Virgin with the Child and Angels in landscape. On wood (33¹/₂ × 27¹/₂ inches). Painted about 1513. Purchased in 1913 from the B. Altman collection.

New York, Metropolitan Museum.

Friedländer, VIII, No. 124.

146. LUCAS VAN LEYDEN, about 1494-1533, in Leyden.

Adoration of the Magi. On wood (10⁵/₈ × 13¹/₄ inches). Painted, according to Friedländer, about 1510; F. also notes that several replicas exist, which are the work of Bruges masters. From the Spanish Gallery, London, and the Martin A. Ryerson collection, Chicago.

Chicago, Illinois, Art Institute.

Friedländer, X, No. 120.

147. PIETER BRUEGHEL THE ELDER, born about 1525 at Brueghel; died 1569 in Brussels.

Open-air wedding-dance. On wood (46³/₄ × 61³/₄ inches). Signed, 1566. Glück mentions a number of copies. Purchased in 1930.

Detroit, Michigan, Institute of Art.

Glück, Breughels Gemälde, Vienna 1932, Plate 24.

148. — Harvest. On wood (46 × 63 inches). Signed, 1565. In the Imperial Gallery, Vienna, until 1805. Purchased in 1930 from the Jacques Doucet collection, Paris.

New York, Metropolitan Museum.

Glück, op. cit., Plate 22.

149. — The unfaithful shepherd. On wood (24 × 33¹/₂ inches). Perhaps identical with a picture mentioned in the 1621 inventory of the Hofburg, Prague. From the Pallavicino-Grimaldi collection.

Philadelphia, Pennsylvania, John G. Johnson Collection.

Glück, op. cit., Plate 37.

150. JAN SANDERS VAN HEMESSEN, born about 1504 at Hemmixem, near Antwerp; died between 1555 and 1566 at Harlem.

"Take up thy bed and walk." On wood 42¹/₂ × 30 inches). Discovered about 1925.

New York, Chester Dale Collection.

Belvedere, 1929, No. 9, p. 40.

151. JAN GOSSAERT called MABUSE, born about 1478 at Maubeuge; died 1535-6 at Antwerp. Anna van Bergen, Marquise de Veere (1492 to 1541). On wood (20⁷/₈ × 17³/₄ inches). There is another version in the P. Lehmann collection, New York. The Boston version was purchased as a Jan Scorel in 1895 from the Bonomi-Cereda collection.

Boston, Massachusetts, Isabella Stewart Gardner Museum.

Friedländer, VIII, No. 76.

152. PETER PAUL RUBENS, born 1577 at Siegen (Westphalia); died 1640 at Antwerp.

Count Heinrich von Bergh. On canvas (45 × 45 inches). Additions at the top and at each side; the name was also added subsequently. Painted about 1630. Since the 18ᵗʰ century the sitter had been wrongly described as Thomas Howard, Earl of Arundel, but this was corrected by Oldenbourg. Acquired in 1898 from the collection of the Earl of Warwick, Warwick Castle.

Boston, Massachusetts, Isabella Stewart Gardner Museum.

Klassiker der Kunst⁴, 88.

153. ANTONIS MOR, born about 1512 at Utrecht; died 1576-77 at Antwerp.

Queen Mary of England (1516-1558). On wood (44 × 32³/₄ inches). Painted in 1554 on the occasion of the Queen's marriage to King Philip II of Spain. Numerous replicas, of which one in the Prado is likewise described as the original. Acquired in 1901 from the collection of Lord Stafford-Jerningham.

Boston, Massachusetts, Isabella Stewart Gardner Museum.

154. PETER PAUL RUBENS, see above, No. 152.

Samson and Delilah. Wood (20 × 25¹/₂ inches). Sketch which amplifies the composition of the painting in the Ältere Pinakothek, Munich. Formerly attributed to Van Dyck. From the F. T. Sabin collection, London.

Chicago, Illinois, Art Institute.

Catalogue of A Century of Progress, Exhibition of Paintings, etc., 1933, No. 77.

155. — Wolf and Fox Hunt. On canvas (96 × 148½ inches). Probably painted, according to John Smith (Catalogue Raisonné, II, p. 273), for General Legranes, a subordinate of the Marchese Spinola. According to Rooses (IV, No. 341), with participation of pupils. Acquired in 1910 from the collection of Baron Ashburton.

New York, Metropolitan Museum.

Klassiker der Kunst[4], *112.*

156. ANTHONY VAN DYCK, born 1599 at Antwerp; died 1641 in London.

Paola Adorno, Marchesa di Brignole-Sale, with her son. On canvas (74½ × 55 inches). Painted about 1625 at Genoa. The most celebrated of the portraits which Van Dyck painted of this lady. From the collection of the Earl of Warwick, Warwick Castle.

Elkins Park, Pennsylvania, Joseph Widener Collection.

Klassiker der Kunst[2], *181.*

157. — Marchesa Elena Grimaldi, wife of the Marchese Nicola Cattaneo. On canvas (96¾ × 67¾ inches). Probably painted in 1623 at Genoa. From Palazzo Cattaneo.

Elkins Park, Pennsylvania, Joseph Widener Collection.

Klassiker der Kunst[2], *187.*

158. — Helena Dubois, née Tromper. On canvas (39⅜ × 32¾ inches). The picture is dated about 1631; its pendant, representing the painter Hendrik Dubois, is in the Städelsches Institut at Frankfurt am Main. Purchased from the collection of Prince Demidoff, Pratolino.

Chicago, Illinois, Art Institute.

Klassiker der Kunst[2], *287.*

159. — James Stuart, Duke of Lennox (1612-1655). On canvas (84¾ × 49¼ inches). A late picture, of which many preliminary studies and replicas or copies exist. From the collection of Lord Methuen. Purchased in 1888.

New York, Metropolitan Museum.

Klassiker der Kunst[2], *411.*

160. JAN LYS, born about 1600 at Oldenburg; died 1629 at Venice.

The Satyr and the Peasant. On canvas (52⅜ × 65⅜ inches). Formerly attributed to Velázquez, but assigned to Lys by Oldenbourg (Jan Lys, Rome, 1921, plate XVII, p. 10).

Elkins Park, Pennsylvania, Joseph Widener Collection.

161 a. FRANS HALS, born 1584 (?) at Antwerp; died 1664 at Haarlem.

Fishergirl. On canvas (31⅛ × 26⅜ inches). According to Valentiner, painted in 1635. From

the collection of Baron de Beurnonville, Purchased in 1881.

Brooklyn, New York, Museum of Art.

Klassiker der Kunst, p. 117.

161 b. — The Flute-player. On canvas (25½ × 25½ inches). Signed. According to Valentiner, painted about 1629-30. Another, slightly different version is in the collection of the Baroness Hirsch de Gerenth, Paris. From the collection of Lady de Clifford.

Toledo, Ohio, Museum of Art.

Klassiker der Kunst, 78.

162. CORNELIS DE VOS, born about 1585 at Hulst; died 1651 at Antwerp.

Mother and Children. On canvas (51 × 41 inches). Purchased in 1909.

New York, Metropolitan Museum.

163. FRANS HALS, see above, No. 161 a.

Jonkheer Ramp and his Mistress. On wood (41¼ × 30¾ inches). Signed, 1623. From the Pourtalès collection, Paris, and the B. Altman collection, New York.

New York, Metropolitan Museum.

Klassiker der Kunst, 23.

164. — Portrait of a Gentleman. On canvas (43 × 31¼ inches). About 1650. Pendant to the portrait of a lady in the La Case collection at the Louvre. From the collection of Earl Amherst, Sevenoaks.

Elkins Park, Pennsylvania, Joseph Widener Collection.

Klassiker der Kunst, 42.

165. — Michael de Wael (?). On canvas (46¼ × 29½ inches). For the sitter Valentiner suggests Tileman Roosterman. (An Exhibition of Fifty Paintings by Frans Hals, Detroit, 1935, No. 22.) Painted about 1634. From the Charles Pillet collection, Paris.

Cincinnati, Ohio, Taft Museum.

Klassiker der Kunst, 113.

166. — Woman with a prayer-book. On canvas (48 × 38½ inches). Signed, 1648. Pendant to the portrait of a gentleman in a private collection at New York.

Boston, Massachusetts, Museum of Fine Art.

Klassiker der Kunst, 224.

167. REMBRANDT, born 1606 at Leyden; died 1669 at Amsterdam.

Portrait of a Man holding a letter. On canvas (47⅝ × 37 inches). Painted about 1662. From the collection of Earl Wimborne, Canford Manor.

Elkins Park, Pennsylvania, Joseph Widener Collection.

Bode, No. 487.

168. — Portrait of a Man. On canvas ($47^1/_4 \times 37$ inches). Signed, 1637. From the W. A. Clark collection, Washington.

Washington, D. C., Corcoran Gallery of Art.

Bode, No. 225.

169. — Portrait of a Married Couple. On canvas ($50^3/_8 \times 42^1/_4$ inches). Signed, 1633. Acquired in 1898 from the Francis Pelham Clinton-Hope collection.

Boston, Massachusetts, Isabella Stewart Gardner Museum.

Bode, No. 99.

170. — Landscape with obelisk. On wood ($21^5/_8 \times 28$ inches). Signed, 1638 (?). From the von Rath collection, Budapest; purchased in 1900.

Boston, Massachusetts, Isabella Stewart Gardner Museum.

Bode, No. 250.

171. — Polish Horseman. On canvas ($45^1/_4 \times 52^3/_8$ inches). About 1655. From the collection of Count Tarnowski, Dzikow.

New York, Frick Art Museum.

Bode, No. 466.

172. — Self-portrait. On canvas ($50^3/_4 \times 49^3/_4$ inches). Signed, 1658.

New York, Frick Art Museum.

Bode, No. 428.

173. — Lucretia. On canvas ($41^1/_2 \times 36^1/_4$ inches). Dated 1666. From the H. V. Jones collection.

Minneapolis, Minnesota, Institute of Arts.

Das unbekannte Meisterwerk, 55.

174. -- Girl behind a door. On canvas ($39^3/_8 \times 33$ inches). Signed, 1645. From the M. A. Ryerson collection, Chicago.

Chicago, Illinois, Art Institute.

Bode, No. 301.

175. — Magdalena van Loo. On canvas ($39 \times 32^1/_2$ inches). Signed, about 1668. The pendant to this picture, representing Titus, is in the same collection. From the collection of Prince Yussupoff, Leningrad.

Elkins Park, Pennsylvania, Joseph Widener Collection.

Bode, No. 490.

176. — St. Bartholomew. On canvas ($49^3/_4 \times 39^1/_2$ inches).

New York, Mrs. Henry Goldman Collection.

Bode, No. 591.

177. — Aristotle (Virgil?). On canvas ($54^3/_4 \times 53^3/_8$ inches). Signed, 1653.

New York, Erickson Collection.

Bode, No. 385.

178. — Pilate washing his hands. On canvas ($49^1/_4 \times 52^3/_8$ inches). About 1665. From the Benjamin Altman collection.

New York, Metropolitan Museum.

Bode, No. 532.

179. — The Mill. On canvas ($33^7/_8 \times 40^3/_8$ inches). About 1650. The authenticity of this beautiful landscape is often doubted, but none of the names suggested instead of Rembrandt's is convincing. From the collection of the Marquess of Lansdowne, Bowood.

Elkins Park, Pennsylvania, Joseph Widener Collection.

Bode, No. 345.

180. — Old Woman cutting her nails. On canvas ($49^5/_8 \times 39^3/_8$ inches). Signed, 1658. The style of the picture is rather reminiscent of Carel Fabritius. From the Benjamin Altman collection.

New York, Metropolitan Museum.

Bode, No. 477.

181 FERDINAND BOL, born about 1616 at Dordrecht; died 1860 at Amsterdam.

Girl at the window. On canvas ($49^3/_8 \times 31^1/_4$ inches). Signed, 1663.

Toledo, Ohio, Museum of Art.

182. JAN STEEN, born 1626 at Leyden; died there in 1679.

Moses bringing forth water from the rock. On canvas ($37 \times 39^3/_8$ inches). Signed. Purchased in 1894 from the collection of Baron Königswarter, Vienna.

Philadelphia, Pennsylvania, John G. Johnson Collection.

Hofstede de Groot, I, 9.

183. PIETER DE HOOCH, born 1629 at Rotterdam; died about 1683 at Amsterdam.

Skittles-players. On canvas ($26 \times 28^3/_4$ inches). According to Valentiner, painted between 1665 and 1668; the same author mentions two other versions. From the collection of the Duchesse de Doudeauville.

St. Louis, Missouri, City Art Museum.

Klassiker der Kunst, 82.

184. — Woman and Child in a courtyard. On canvas ($28^3/_4 \times 25^1/_2$ inches). Signed, Painted about 1656.

Elkins Park, Pennsylvania, Joseph Widener Collection.

Klassiker der Kunst, 39.

185. JAN VERMEER, 1629-1683, in Delft.

Young Woman with water-jug. On canvas ($17^3/_4 \times 15^3/_8$ inches). From the collection of

Lord Powerscourt. Presented to the Museum in 1888 by Henry G. Marquand.

New York, Metropolitan Museum.

Plietzsch, No. 12.

186. — Sleeping Girl. On canvas (33$^1/_2$ × 29 inches). Signed. From the Rudolph Kann collection, Paris, and the B. Altman collection, New York.

New York, Metropolitan Museum.

Plietzsch, No. 4.

187. — Woman weighing pearls. On canvas (16$^7/_8$ × 15 inches). Signed. From the Ségur-Périer collection, Paris.

Elkins Park, Pennsylvania, Joseph Widener Collection.

188. — Lace-maker. According to Valentiner, painted about the beginning of the 1660's. From the R. Right Collection.

Washington, D. C., Museum.

189. — Girl with flute. On wood (7$^7/_8$ × 7$^1/_8$ inches). Discovered in 1906 by Dr. Abraham Bredius in the house of Jonkheer de Grez, Brussels.

Elkins Park, Pennsylvania, Joseph Widener Collection.

Plietzsch, No. 20.

190. — Head of a smiling Girl. From the Rohde collection.

Washington, D. C., Museum.

191. AERT DE GELDER, 1645-1727, in Dordrecht.

Bust-portrait of a girl. On canvas (26 × 20$^7/_8$ inches). According to Lilienfeld, painted about 1690. From the collection of Mr. H. Ker-Colville, Jr., Bellport Towers, England.

Chicago, Illinois, Art Institute.

192. JACOB VAN RUYSDAEL, born 1628-29 at Haarlem; died there in 1682.

Forest Landscape. On canvas (41 × 50 inches). Signed. Painted about 1660-65. From the collection of Sir Hugh Hume Campbell, Bart., London.

Elkins Park, Pennsylvania, Joseph Widener Collection.

Rosenberg, Ruysdael, No. 374.

193. — Wheatfields. On canvas (39$^7/_8$ × 50$^5/_8$ inches). Signed. From the Moritz Kann collection; B. Altman collection, New York.

New York, Metropolitan Museum.

Rosenberg, Ruysdael, No. 86 a.

194. MEINDERT HOBBEMA, born 1638 at Amsterdam; died there in 1709.

Landscape with Cottages. On canvas (36$^5/_8$ × 40$^1/_2$ inches). To judge by its similarity to the picture in the Frick Collection, probably painted about 1665. The figures are perhaps by Lingelbach. From the collection of Lady Carnarvon, London.

Washington, D. C., Museum.

195. CONRAD VON SOEST, active in the early fifteenth century in Westphalia.

Coronation of the Virgin. On wood (26$^3/_8$ × 20$^1/_4$ inches). Purchased in 1929 from the Loeb-Caldendorf collection.

Cleveland, Ohio, Museum of Art.

196. JOHANN KOERBECKE, active 1446-1491 at Münster, Westphalia.

Annunciation. Transferred from wood to canvas (36$^1/_4$ × 24$^5/_8$ inches). Originally this was probably a part of the 1457 altar-piece of the Virgin in the abbey of Marienfeld, Westphalia; the remaining fourteen panels can be traced in various collections. At Marienfeld until 1804; later in the Martin A. Ryerson collection, Chicago.

Chicago, Illinois, Art Institute.

W. Hugelshofer, in Cicerone, 1930, pp. 371 seq.

197. MASTER OF THE AUGSBURG VISITATION, last quarter of fifteenth century.

Crucifixion. On wood (74$^1/_2$ × 41 inches). Originally attributed to Rueland Frueauf. Acquired in 1922.

Detroit, Michigan, Institute of Art.

Buchner, in Beiträge zur Geschichte der Deutschen Kunst, II, pp. 56 seq.

198. SCHOOL OF ULM, about 1470.

A Pair of Lovers. On wood (25$^3/_8$ × 15$^3/_8$ inches). Stylistically akin to the Master of the House-book and the anonymous master E. S., but not derived from either of these. Purchased in 1932 from the Schützenberger collection, Mulhouse.

Cleveland, Ohio, Museum of Art.

Bulletin, 1932, p. 127.

199. SOUTH GERMAN SCHOOL, about 1491.

Portrait of a Young Man. On wood (19 × 13 inches). Signed: 1491 H. H., the letters having been added later, perhaps an attempted forgery of Holbein's signature. The attribution to the Franconian school in the catalogue is attractive; Wehle (Bulletin, 1924, p. 61) is still more definite and would like to assign it to the master of the St. Augustine altar-piece at Nürnberg. Purchased in 1923 from the castle of Nijenrode.

New York, Metropolitan Museum.

200. MASTER OF ST. SEVERIN, active in the early sixteenth century at Cologne.

Beheading of John the Baptist. On wood (50 × 39$^3/_8$ inches). Part of a triptych painted in

1511, of which other wings are to be found in the Chicago gallery. According to Reiners (Die Kölner Malerschule, 1925, A. 254), may be a workshop painting.

Boston, Massachusetts, Museum of Fine Arts.

201. ALBRECHT DÜRER, 1471-1528, in Nürnberg.
St. Anne with the Virgin and Child. On wood (23⅝ × 19¾ inches). Signed, 1519. This picture, of which many replicas exist, was rejected by the Schleissheim gallery because its authenticity was doubted, but this is generally accepted since the appearance of Wustmann's article in Zeitschrift für Bildende Kunst, new series, XXI, p. 52. From the Jean de Couriss collection, Odessa; B. Altman collection, New York.

New York, Metropolitan Museum.

Klassiker der Kunst⁴, 64.

202. — Portrait of a Young Man, who, according to tradition, confirmed by the dates on the picture, is Christoph or Albrecht Scheurl. On wood (17¾ × 11¾ inches). Painted in 1504. This recently discovered and very important portrait was attributed by Gustav Glück to Dürer, but as I have not seen the original, I am unable to form a definite opinion as to the attribution, but am more inclined to give the painting to Hans Baldung Grien.

Indianapolis, Indiana, G. H. A. Clowes Collect.

203. — Portrait of a young man. On wood (16 × 12½ inches). Signed with monogram and dated 1507. Although a number of critics, especially Winkler (Klassiker der Kunst, p. 414) and Friedländer (Das unbekannte Meisterwerk, T. 62) endorse the ascription to Dürer, Buchner and Tietze (Der reife Dürer, 11/2, A 202) ascribe it to Hans Schäuffelein, whose style at the beginning of the XVI Century closely resembled that of his teacher Dürer. A closely related portrait may be found in the National Museum at Warshaw. From the Count Bondi Coll., Ericsberg.

Washington, D. C., Museum.

204. LUCAS CRANACH the Elder, born 1472 at Kronach, Franconia; died 1553 at Weimar.
Young Man with rosary. On wood (19 × 14 inches). According to Friedländer-Rosenberg (Die Gemälde des Lucas Cranach, 1932, No. 99), painted about 1510-12. From the H. O. Havemeyer collection.

New York, Metropolitan Museum.

205. — Portrait of a Young Lady. On wood. Signed.

New York, John Schiff Collection.

206. HANS VON KULMBACH, born about 1476 at Kulmbach, Franconia; died 1522 at Nürnberg.
Girl with cat at a window. On wood (7⅛ × 5½ inches). Spurious Dürer monogram and date

1508. On the back is the portrait of a young man. Formerly supposed to be by Wolf Traut, but F. Winkler brought forward better reasons for assigning it to Kulmbach. Purchased in 1917 from the collection of Prince Santangelo, Naples.

New York, Metropolitan Museum.

207. LUCAS CRANACH the Elder, see above, No. 204.
The Judgement of Paris. On wood (19¾ × 14 inches). The picture exists in several versions, of which that in Karlsruhe is the most closely related. From the ducal collection in Gotha.

St. Louis, Missouri, City Art Museum.

Friedländer-Rosenberg, No. 210c.

208. CHRISTOPH AMBERGER, 1500-63, at Augsburg.
Portrait of an elderly Man. On wood (16½ × 13⅜ inches). From the collection of the Countess of Dartrey, Monaghan, Ireland.

Chicago, Illinois, Art Institute.

209. HANS MALER ZU SCHWAZ, active about 1519-1529 at Schwaz, Tyrol.
Ulrich Fugger (1490-1525), the Augsburg banker. On wood (12¾ × 15¾ inches). On the back, the date 1525. A study from nature for the portrait of Fugger in the possession of Count Franz Thun (Wiener Jahrbuch, XXV, p. 240, communication by Dr. Otto Benesch). From the von Heyl collection, Darmstadt; B. Altman collection, New York.

New York, Metropolitan Museum.

210. BARTEL BEHAM, born 1502 at Nürnberg; died 1540, probably in Italy.
Leonhard von Eck, Bavarian Chancellor, 1480 to 1550. On wood (19¾ × 14¾ inches). Coincides in its essentials with Beham's engraving (B. 64) of 1527, which must be the graphic transcription either of the picture or of the drawing on which it was based. From the Weber collection, Hamburg.

New York, Metropolitan Museum.

Katalog der Sammlung Weber, No. 57.

211. HANS BURGKMAIR, 1473-1531, at Augsburg.
Portrait of an Architect. On wood (13 × 9½ inches). Signed, 1507. From the collection of Count Florio, Udine.

New York, Ernst Rosenfeld Collection.

Burgkmair Exhibition, 1832, No. 9.

212. MASTER OF THE ANGERER PORTRAITS, active in the Tyrol at the beginning of the 16th century.
Portrait of a beardless man. On wood (16 × 12 inches). Formerly attributed to Christoph Amberger.

St. Louis, Missouri, City Art Museum.

213. HANS HOLBEIN THE YOUNGER, born 1497 at Augsburg; died 1543 in London.

Benedikt von Hertenstein, born about 1495, Grand Councillor 1517, fell in 1522. On paper, mounted on wood ($15^3/_8 \times 11^3/_8$ inches). Signed, 1517. Purchased in 1906 from a private collection in England.

New York, Metropolitan Museum.

Klassiker der Kunst, 15.

214. — Lady Elizabeth Rich. On wood ($17^1/_2 \times 13^3/_8$ inches). There is a study for the picture at Windsor. From the collection of Herbert Croft, Bishop of Hereford; B. Altman collection, New York.

New York, Metropolitan Museum.

215. — Lady Margaret Butts. On wood ($18^1/_8 \times 14^1/_2$ inches). Painted in 1541-3. Pendant to the portrait of Sir William Butts in the same collection. Purchased in 1899 from the W. H. Pole-Carew collection, Antony, Cornwall.

Boston, Massachusetts, Isabella Stewart Gardner Collection.

Klassiker der Kunst, 133.

216. — Dirk Berch, of Cologne. On wood ($21^1/_8 \times 16^3/_4$ inches). Dated 1536. First reproduced by P. Ganz (Burlington Magazine, XX, p. 31). There is an unfinished copy at Munich. Acquired from the collection of Lord Leconfield, Petworth.

Washington, D. C., Museum.

Klassiker der Kunst, 401.

217. ALBRECHT DÜRER.

Portrait of a beardless Man. On wood ($19^3/_4 \times 12^1/_2$ inches). Signed, 1521. The sitter has been variously identified, recently as Lazarus Ravensburger. Occasional doubts as to the authenticity of the picture were due to its bad state of preservation. It was cleaned in 1935. Purchased in 1902 from the J. T. Dobie collection.

Boston, Massachusetts, Isabella Stewart Gardner Museum.

Klassiker der Kunst[4]*, 71; Hendy, Catalogue, pp. 132 seq.*

218. ENGLISH SCHOOL, 1598, style of Marcus Gheeraerts the Younger.

Portrait of a Lady with her child. On wood. Cf. the anonymous portrait of Robert Devereux, 2nd Earl of Essex, painted in 1599, at Minneapolis (Bulletin, 1929), and also the portraits of Catherine, Countess of Nottingham and Lady E. Howard by Gheeraerts (Belvedere, 1927, 164). Purchased in 1935.

Providence, R. I., Rhode Island School of Design.

Bulletin, April 1935.

219. WILLIAM HOGARTH, born 1697 in London; died 1764 in Leicester Fields.

Lady and Child. On canvas (30×25 inches). From the W. A. Clark collection.

Washington, D. C., Corcoran Gallery of Art.

220 a. — William James. On canvas ($29^1/_2 \times 24^1/_2$ inches). Signed, 1744. Pendant to 220 b.

Worcester, Massachusetts, Art Museum.

220 b. — Mrs. William James. Pendant 220 a.

Worcester, Massachusetts, Art Museum.

221. — The Price Family. On canvas ($40 \times 62^1/_2$ inches). Purchased in 1920 from the collection of Thomas Price, London.

New York, Metropolitan Museum.

Bulletin, 1920, p. 89.

222. JOSEPH HIGHMORE, born 1692 in London; died 1780 at Canterbury.

Portrait of a Gentleman. On canvas.

San Marino, California, Huntington Art Gallery.

223. THOMAS GAINSBOROUGH, born 1727 at Sudbury; died 1788 in London.

Mrs. Mary Graham (1752-92). On canvas ($35^1/_4 \times 27^1/_4$ inches). Painted in 1775-6. There is a full-length portrait of the same lady, dressed as a maidservant, in the National Gallery, London. From the collection of A. G. Maxtone-Graham, Cultoquhey, Crieff., Perthshire.

Elkins Park, Pennsylvania, Joseph Widener Collection.

224. — The Artist's Daughter Margaret. On canvas ($18^1/_2 \times 14^3/_4$ inches). Either a study for or a repetition of one of the figures in the double portrait of his daughters in the Victoria & Albert Museum, London. Painted about 1757-8. From the Morris K. Jesup collection. Purchased in 1915.

New York, Metropolitan Museum.

Bulletin, 1915, p. 194.

225. — The Artist's Daughters Margaret and Mary. On canvas (50×40 inches). Both the girls appear older than in the double portrait in the Victoria & Albert Museum. About 1765.

Worcester, Massachusetts, Art Museum.

226. SIR JOSUAH REYNOLDS, born 1723 at Plympton Earl, Plymouth; died 1792 in London.

Theresa Parker (1775-1856). On canvas (30×25 inches). Painted in 1787. Purchased in 1926 from the collection of the Earl of Morley.

San Marino, California, Huntington, Art Gallery.

227. THOMAS GAINSBOROUGH, see above No. 223.

The Blue Boy. Jonathan Buttall (1756-1805), son of a blacksmith and ironmonger (70 × 48½ inches). Two replicas of this, the most popular of all Gainsborough's portraits, are known. Purchased in 1921 from the collection of the Duke of Westminster, Grosvenor House.

San Marino, California, Huntington Art Gallery.

228. SIR JOSHUA REYNOLDS, see above, No. 226.

Nancy Parsons, Viscountess Maynard (1734 to 1840). On canvas (35¾ × 28 inches). Painted in 1769. This well-known beauty was also painted by Gainsborough. From the collection of Frances, Countess of Warwick.

New York, Jules S. Bache Collection.

229. GEORGE ROMNEY, born 1734 at Beckside, Dalton-in-Furness; died 1802 at Kendal.

Mrs. Charlotte Davenport. On canvas (30 × 24¾ inches). Painted in 1777. From the Bromley-Davenport collection.

Washington, D. C., Museum.

230. SIR JOSHUA REYNOLDS, see above, No. 226.

Lady Diana Crosbie (1756-1814). On canvas (93 × 58 inches). Painted in 1777. Purchased in 1923 from the collection of Baron Glenconner.

San Marino, California, Huntington Art Gallery.

231. — Mrs. Siddons as the Tragic Muse. On canvas (93 × 56¾ inches). Signed. Painted in 1784. A celebrated masterpiece, of which several repetitions exist. Purchased in 1921 from the collection of the Duke of Westminster, Grosvenor House.

San Marino, California, Huntington Art Gallery.

232. SIR HENRY RAEBURN, born 1756 at Stockbridge, Edinburgh; died 1823 at Edinburgh.

The Elphinstone Children. On canvas (77½ × 60¼ inches).

Cincinnati, Ohio, Art Museum.

233. JOHN HOPPNER, born 1758 in Whitechapel; died 1810 in London.

The Artist's Three Children. On canvas (60 × 50 inches). Reproduced in mezzotint by James Ward in 1799. Purchased in 1893 from the Hoppner family.

Elkins Park, Pennsylvania, Joseph Widener Collection.

234. SIR THOMAS LAWRENCE, born 1769 at Bristol; died 1830 in London.

William Locke (1732-1810). On canvas (28¾ × 24 inches). Painted in 1790. Purchased in 1920.

Boston, Massachusetts, Museum of Fine Arts.

235. THOMAS GAINSBOROUGH, see above, No. 223.

The Cottage Door. On canvas (56¾ × 46 inches). Painted 1776-8. Exhibited at the Royal Academy in 1780. Purchased in 1922 from the collection of the Duke of Westminster, Grosvenor House.

San Marino, California, Huntington Art Gallery.

236. JOHN CONSTABLE, born 1776 at East Bergholt, Suffolk; died 1837 in London.

Hampstead Heath. On canvas (24 × 30¼ inches). From the McFaddon collection.

Philadelphia, Pa., Pennsylvania Museum of Art.

237. — Weymouth Bay. On canvas (20¾ × 30 inches). From the collection of Mr. and Mrs. C. Loring. Acquired in 1930.

Boston, Massachusetts, Museum of Fine Arts.

238. RICHARD PARKES BONINGTON, born 1802 at Arnold, near Nottingham; died 1828 in London.

Seacoast in Normandy. On canvas (24 × 33 inches). From the McFaddon collection.

Philadelphia, Pa., Pennsylvania Museum of Art.

239. — Santa Maria della Salute, Venice. On canvas (12¾ × 21⅝ inches). Copy of Canaletto's picture in the Louvre.

Worcester, Massachusetts, Art Museum.

Bulletin, July 1923.

240. JOSEPH MALLORD WILLIAM TURNER, 1775-1851, in London.

The Grand Canal, Venice. On canvas.

Baltimore, Maryland, Walters Art Gallery.

241. WILLIAM BLAKE, 1757-1827, in London.

Christ and the Woman taken in adultery. Water-colour on paper (12½ × 14¼ inches).

Boston, Massachusetts, Museum of Fine Arts.

Figgis, The Paintings of William Blake, London, 1925, Plate 44.

242. SOUTHERN FRENCH SCHOOL, about 1400.

The Virgin and Child, with the Blessed Peter of Luxembourg presenting a donor. On wood (21½ × 16½ inches). Peter of Luxembourg, 1369-89, was beatified in 1525; the coat of arms above his head is that of Luxembourg. The identification is upheld by the similarity of the portrait of the Blessed Peter in the museum at Avignon.

Worcester, Massachusetts, Art Museum.

Bulletin, XIV, April 1923.

243. SOUTHERN FRENCH SCHOOL, early 15th century.

A Bishop-Saint with kneeling donor. On wood (67¾ × 41¾ inches). The attributions hesitate between the Southern French and Catalan schools. From the chapel of the Counts of Chatiner d'Esterre, near Toulouse.

Cleveland, Ohio, Museum of Art.

Bulletin, April 1928 and March 1930.

244. SOUTHERN FRENCH SCHOOL, about 1450.

St. Jerome translating the Gospels. On wood (63 × 31½ inches). Winkler relates this picture to the Aix Annunciation, but dates it before Nicolas Froment. From the Lambert collection, Oudenarde.

New York, Mogmar Art Foundation.

Das unbekannte Meisterwerk, No. 71.

245. NORTHERN FRENCH SCHOOL, about 1460.

Mourning for Christ. On wood (16¾ × 11¼ inches). The attribution and dating are J. M. Friedländer's.

Chicago, Illinois, Max Epstein Collection; on loan to the Art Institute.

246. SIMON MARMION, born 1425 at Valenciennes; died 1489; active in Northern and Flanders.

St. Jerome with the Canonicus Busleyden. On wood (26 × 20 inches).

Philadelphia, Pennsylvania, John G. Johnson Collection.

247. BURGUNDIAN SCHOOL, about 1500.

The Grand Bastard of Burgundy as donor with a Bishop-Saint. On wood (41 × 30¼ inches). A fragment, of which the pendant, a portrait of Guillemette de Vergy with her Patroness, is in the School of Design at Providence, Rhode Island. It has been impossible to localize exactly these two fragments, which come from the Hainauer collection, Berlin.

Worcester, Massachusetts, Art Museum.

248. THE MASTER OF MOULINS, perhaps Jean Perréal, born about 1455; died 1553; court painter in Lyons.

Portrait of a Man praying. On wood (13⅜ × 9½ inches). The attribution wavers between the French and Flemish schools; recently Baldass has assigned it to the Flemish master Michiel.

New York, Ernst Rosenfeld Collection.

249. FONTAINEBLEAU SCHOOL, middle of 16th century.

Diane de Poitiers at her toilet. On wood. The portrait has been attributed to François Clouet, owing to the similarity to the portrait of Diane in Sir Herbert Cook's collection, Richmond, but it obviously belongs to a later stage of stylistic development.

Worcester, Massachusetts, Art Museum.

250. LOUIS LENAIN, 1593-1648, at Laon.

Peasants in Landscape. On canvas (16¼ × 21⅝ inches). The old woman on the right is found again almost exactly the same in Louis Lenain's "Saying Grace" at the National Gallery, London. From the George Wilbraham collection, Northwich, Cheshire.

Hartford, Connecticut, Wadsworth Atheneum.

Paul Fierens, Les Lenain, 1933, pp. 28, 30, 62; Plate XXXIII.

251 a. PIERRE DUBORDIEU, born 1609-10 at Ile-Bouchard, Touraine; died after 1678, probably at Leyden.

Portrait of a Young Woman. On canvas (22½ × 19¼ inches). Identified by Dr. Hans Schneider and dated about 1640 by Martin. From the Auspitz collection, Vienna.

Chicago, Illinois, Art Institute.

W. Martin, in Burlington Magazine, XLI, p. 217.

251 b. FRENCH SCHOOL, about 1660.

Portrait of an unknown Lady. On canvas (31½ × 24¾ inches). Friedländer has suggested Philippe de Champaigne (1602-74), an attribution which seems to tally with the general tendency of this picture.

New York, G. L. Winthrop Collection.

252. NICOLAS POUSSIN, born 1593 at Villières, Normandy; died 1665 in Rome.

Triumph of Neptune and Amphitrite. On canvas (45 × 58 inches). One of the four Triumphs which Poussin painted in 1639 for Cardinal de Richelieu. From the Hermitage, Leningrad.

Philadelphia, Pa., Pennsylvania Museum of Art.

Granhoff, No. 87.

253. — Blind Orion seeking the rising sun. On canvas (46¾ × 72 inches). Painted in 1658 for Michel Passart. Purchased in 1924 from the collection of Baron Methuen.

New York, Metropolitan Museum.

Bulletin, 1924, p. 100; Borenius, in Burlington Magazine, 1931, p. 207.

254. NICOLAS DE LARGILLIÈRE, 1656-1746, in Paris.

The Marquis de Montespan. Signed, 1712. On canvas (53 × 41¼ inches). From the Archer M. Huntington collection.

San Francisco, California, Palace of the Legion of Honour.

Exhibition of French Painting, San Francisco, 1934, 32.

255. ANTOINE WATTEAU, born 1684 at Valenciennes; died 1721 in Paris.

"Mezzetin." On canvas (21⅝ × 16⅞ inches). Painted about 1716-18; engraved by Audran. Known to have belonged to Julienne. Purchased in 1935 from the Hermitage, Leningrad.

New York, Metropolitan Museum.

Klassiker der Kunst, 41.

256. NICOLAS LANCRET, 1690-1743, in Paris.

The Dancer Camargo, dancing in a park. On canvas (30¹/₄ × 42 inches). From the New Palace, Potsdam.

Washington, D. C., Museum.

257. JEAN-BAPTISTE-SIMÉON CHARDIN, 1699 to 1779, in Paris.

Man blowing bubbles. On canvas (23⁵/₈ × 25¹/₂ inches). Signed. There is another version in the David Weill collection, Paris.

Kansas City, William Rockhill Nelson Gallery of Art.

Georges Wildenstein, Chardin, No. 136.

258. FRANCOIS-HUBERT DROUAIS, 1727-1775, in Paris.

Madame d'Aiguirande. On canvas.

Cleveland, Ohio, John L. Severance Collection.

259. MAURICE QUENTIN DE LA TOUR, 1704 to 1788, at Saint-Quentin.

Madame de Mondonville. On canvas (25¹/₂ × 21¹/₄ inches). Preparatory sketch at Saint-Quentin.

St. Louis, Missouri, City Art Museum.

260. JEAN-HONORÉ FRAGONARD, born 1732 at Grasse; died 1806 in Paris.

The Rendezvous. On canvas (142 × 112 inches). One of a series of five panels which Fragonard painted in 1770-72 for Madame Dubarry and which in 1790-1 he took with him to the Maison Maubert at Grasse. Acquired in 1915 from the J. Pierpont Morgan collection.

New York, Frick Art Museum.

Portalis, Fragonard, p. 284.

261. — The Love-letter. On canvas (31 × 27¹/₈ inches). The girl is Boucher's daughter, before her marriage to Monsieur de Cuviller, whose name is written on the letter. From the Ernest Bardac collection.

New York, Jules S. Bache Collection.

Portalis, Fragonard, p. 272.

262. LOUIS-JACQUES DAVID, born 1748 in Paris; died 1825 in Brussels.

Mademoiselle Charlotte du Val d'Ognes. On canvas (63³/₈ × 50³/₈ inches). Painted about 1795. Acquired in 1917 from the Isaac D. Fletcher collection.

New York, Metropolitan Museum.

Bulletin, XIII/3, p. 59.

263. JEAN - AUGUSTE - DOMINIQUE INGRES, born 1780 at Montauban; died 1867 in Paris.

Portrait of a Gentleman. On canvas (29¹/₂ × 22³/₄ inches). In the background, the Colosseum, from which, and from the manner, we may assume that the picture was painted in Ingres' Roman period (before 1814). From the H. O. Havemeyer collection, New York.

New York, Metropolitan Museum.

264 a. JEAN-LOUIS-ANDRÉ-THÉODORE GÉRICAULT, born 1791 at Rouen; died 1824 in Paris.

Hercules killing Licas. On canvas. Probably influenced by Canova's group of the same subject, Rome 1815. Signed. Acquired in 1926.

Northampton, Massachusetts, Smith College, Museum of Art.

Bulletin, May 1932.

264 b. — Horseman at the door of an inn ("Au Cheval blanc"). On canvas (22¹/₂ × 18¹/₂ inches).

New York, G. L. Winthrop Collection.

265. EUGÈNE DELACROIX, born 1798 at Charenton-Saint-Maurice; died 1863 in Paris.

Lion-hunt. On canvas (30 × 38³/₈ inches). Signed, 1861. The picture is frequently mentioned in Delacroix's diary. From the collection of Mrs. Potter Palmer, Chicago.

Chicago, Illinois, Art Institute.

266. — Paganini. On canvas (16¹/₄ × 11 inches). Washington, D. C., Phillips Memorial Gallery.

Robaut, No. 386.

267. HONORÉ DAUMIER, born 1808 at Marseilles; died 1879 at Valmondois.

Madame Pipelet. On canvas (18 × 15 inches). Signed. Madame Pipelet was the concierge at the house in Rue Pigalle where Daumier lived in 1840; she also figures in the series of lithographs, "Bohémiens de Paris", 1841.

Providence, R. I., Rhode Island School of Design.

Fuchs, No. 298b.

268. — In the Third Class. On canvas (26³/₈ × 36⁵/₈ inches). Older version of a larger picture which was formerly in the collection of Count Doria. Acquired in 1929 from the H. O. Havemeyer collection.

New York, Metropolitan Museum.

269. — After the Theatre. On canvas (12¹/₂ × 15³/₄ inches). Painted about 1840. From the Richard Owen collection, Paris.

Kansas City, William Rockhill Nelson Gallery of Art.

Fuchs, No. 40.

270. — The Riot (L'Émeute). On canvas (31 × 41 inches). Painted about 1848. Discovered about 1924 and for a time exhibited in the Louvre.

Washington, D. C., Phillips Memorial Gallery.

Arsène Alexandre, in Burlington Magazine, 1924, p. 143.

271. THÉODORE CHASSÉRIAU, born 1819 at Le
Limon, Sainte-Barbe de Samana, San Domingo;
died 1856 in Paris.

Arabian Horsemen carrying away their dead.
On canvas (67 × 98½ inches). Signed, 1850.
Exhibited at the Salon, 1850-1. From the
Pereire collection.

New York, G. L. Winthrop Collection.

Henri Marcel, Chassériau, No. 35.

272. GUSTAVE COURBET, born 1819 at Ornans;
died 1877 at La Tour de Peilz (Switzerland).

The Stag-hunt ("La Curée"). On canvas (38 ×
71 inches). Exhibited in 1857; sold in 1866 to
the Alston Club, Boston.

Boston, Massachusetts, Museum of Fine Arts.

273. — The Amazon, Madame Louise Colet
(poetess, 1810-76). On canvas (45¾ × 35
inches). Signed. Painted about 1856. From the
H. O. Havemeyer collection.

New York, Metropolitan Museum.

274. JEAN-FRANÇOIS MILLET, born 1814 at
Gruchy; died 1875 at Barbizon.

Planting Potatoes. On canvas (32³/₄ × 39³/₈
inches).

Boston, Massachusetts, Museum of Fine Arts.

275. — Farm at Gréville. On canvas (21¼ × 28¾
inches). Signed. Painted in 1871. Purchased in
1931.

Northampton, Massachusetts, Smith College,
Museum of Art.

276. JEAN-BAPTISTE-CAMILLE COROT, 1796
to 1875, in Paris.

Monsieur Abel Osmond, a friend of Corot
who died in 1835. On canvas (21 × 27½
inches). Signed, 1829. From the Pierre Osmond
collection. Acquired in 1922.

New York, Adolph Lewisohn Collection.

Robaut, No. 205, Vol. II, p. 72.

277. — Portrait of a Girl. On canvas (9³/₄ × 8½
inches). Signed, 1859.

New York, Chester Dale Collection.

278. — The Atelier. On wood (24 × 15¼ inches).
Signed. Painted 1865-68. Sold by auc-
tion after Corot's death, 1875, No. 134. Two
variants of the picture are known. Acquired
in 1892.

Elkins Park, Pennsylvania, Joseph Widener
Collection.

Robaut, No. 1558.

279. CHASSÉRIAU, see above, No. 271.

The Fisherman's Wife. On wood (6³/₄ × 4³/₄
inches). Signed. Exhibited at the Salon,
1850-1. From the collection of Baron A. Chassériau, Paris.

Providence, R. I., Rhode Island School of
Design.

Henri Marcel, Chassériau, No. 38.

280. COROT, see above, No. 276.

The Church of Saint-Salvi, at Albi. On canvas
(10 × 11½ inches). Signed. Painted about
1830.

Chicago, Illinois, Art Institute.

281. — Wood-gatherers. On canvas (45 × 65 inches).

Washington, D. C., Corcoran Gallery of Art.

282. ÉDOUARD MANET, 1832-83, in Paris.

Kneeling Monk. On canvas (57½ × 45 inches).
Painted in 1865. From the Jacques Blanche
collection.

Boston, Massachusetts, Museum of Fine Arts.

Duret, No. 62.

283. — The Mocking of Christ. On canvas (74½ ×
57 inches). Signed. Painted in 1865. From the
James Deering collection.

Chicago, Illinois, Art Institute.

Duret, No. 57.

284. — The Son of Madame Lange. On canvas
(45¾ × 28¾ inches). Painted about 1861.
From the collection of Mrs. L. L. Coeburn.

Chicago, Illinois, Art Institute.

285. — Mademoiselle Victorine in Espada costume.
On canvas (65 × 50½ inches). Signed, 1862.
Rejected by the Salon in 1863; exhibited the
same year at the Salon des Refusés. Victorine
Meurend often sat as a model to Manet,
notably for his "Olympia". From the H. O.
Havemeyer collection.

New York, Metropolitan Museum.

Jamot-Wildenstein, Manet, Paris 1932, No. 51.

286. — The dead Toreador. On canvas (29½ ×
60¼ inches). The essential part of a picture
called "Episode from a Bullfight", which was
exhibited at the Salon in 1864, No. 1282; the
other part of the picture is in the collection
of Baron Vitta, Paris. A Spaniard from Lola
de Valence's troupe is said to have been the
model for this figure; noteworthy is the re-
semblance to the "Dead Warrior", purchased
as by Velázquez by the National Gallery,
London, at the W. Pourtalés sale, Paris, 1865.
From the J. B. Faure collection, Paris.

Elkins Park, Pennsylvania, Joseph Widener
Collection.

Duret, No. 51.

287. — In the Boat. On canvas (38¼ × 51¼
inches). Painted about 1874; exhibited at the
Salon in 1879. From the H. O. Havemeyer
collection, New York.

New York, Metropolitan Museum.

Duret, No. 131.

288. CLAUDE MONET, born 1840 in Paris; died 1926 at Ginevry.

The Seine. On canvas (23 × 25³/₄ inches). Signed. From the early period.

New York, Adolph Lewisohn Collection.

289. — Saint-Lazare Station. On canvas (23¹/₂ × 31¹/₂ inches). Signed, 1877. One of a series of pictures of Saint-Lazare Station (a view from outside is in the Rhode Island School of Design, Providence), which were first exhibited at the third Impressionist exhibition in 1877. From the M. A. Ryerson collection, Chicago.

Chicago, Illinois, Art Institute.

290. EDGAR DEGAS, 1834-1917, in Paris.

Achille de Gas in the uniform of a naval officer. On canvas (25¹/₄ × 20 inches). Painted in 1856-7.

New York, Chester Dale Collection.

291. — Madame Gaujelin. On canvas (23⁵/₈ × 17³/₈ inches). Signed, 1867. The sitter refused to accept the picture. There are studies for it in the Kunsthalle, Hamburg, and the Olivier Senn collection, Le Havre. Purchased in 1904 from the Manzi collection, Paris.

Boston, Massachusetts, Isabella Stewart Gardner Museum.

292 a. — Carriage on a race-course in Provence. On canvas (13³/₄ × 20 inches). Signed. Exhibited in 1874. Purchased in 1927 from the Faure collection, Paris.

Boston, Massachusetts, Museum of Fine Arts.

292 b. — Ballet-dancers practising. On canvas (30 × 32 inches). Signed. From the collections of Henri Rouart and H. O. Havemeyer, New York. Acquired in 1929.

New York, Metropolitan Museum.

293. — The Duke and Duchess de Morbilli. On canvas (45³/₄ × 35¹/₄ inches). Signed, 1879. From the L. L. Coeburn collection.

Boston, Massachusetts, Museum of Fine Arts.

294. PIERRE-AUGUSTE RENOIR, born 1841 at Limoges; died 1919 in Paris.

Madame Darras. On canvas (30³/₄ × 24¹/₂ inches). Painted in 1871; pendant to the portrait of an officer in the Dresden gallery.

New York, Adolph Lewisohn Collection.

295. — Woman sewing. On canvas (19¹/₂ × 24 inches). Signed, 1879. From the L. L. Coeburn collection.

Chicago, Illinois, Art Institute.

J. Meier-Graefe, Auguste Renoir, 1929, p. 122, No. 108.

296. — Odalisque. On canvas (27 × 28¹/₂ inches). Signed, 1870.

New York, Chester Dale Collection.

297. — Oarsmen at lunch ("Le Déjeuner des Canotiers"). On canvas (51¹/₄ × 68 inches). Signed, 1881. From the Durand-Ruel collection.

Washington, D. C., Phillips Memorial Gallery.

Meier-Graefe, Renoir, p. 152, No. 137.

298. PAUL CÉZANNE, 1839-1906, at Aix-en-Provence.

Landscape near Aix-en-Provence. On canvas (25³/₄ × 32¹/₄ inches). Purchased in 1929 from the H. O. Havemeyer collection.

New York, Metropolitan Museum.

299. — Card-players. On canvas. Painted in 1892. There is a smaller version in the Stephen C. Clark collection, New York. From the Vollard collection, Paris.

Merion, Pennsylvania, Barnes Foundation.

300. — Youth in a small hat (Cézanne's son). On canvas (25¹/₂ × 21¹/₄ inches). Painted in 1885.

New York, Chester Dale Collection.

301. HENRI TOULOUSE-LAUTREC, born 1864 at Albi; died 1901 at the Château de Malromé (Gironde).

Prostitute. On canvas.

Merion, Pennsylvania, Barnes Foundation.

302. VINCENT VAN GOGH, born 1853 at Groot-Zundert (Holland); died 1890 at Auvers-sur-Oise.

La Mousmée. On canvas (29¹/₈ × 24 inches). Supposed portrait of Mademoiselle Gachet.

New York, Chester Dale Collection.

303. — The Arlésienne. On canvas (36 × 29¹/₈ inches). Portrait of Madame Ginoux. There is another version in the Federn collection, Witkowitz.

New York, Adolph Lewisohn Collection.

De la Faille, Plate 489.

304. GEORGES SEURAT, 1859-91, in Paris.

Sunday on the island of the Grand-Jatte. On canvas (80³/₄ × 120 inches). Painted in 1884-6. Numerous drawings and painter studies for various parts of the composition exist. From the F. C. Bartlett collection.

Chicago, Illinois, Art Institute.

INDEX OF ARTISTS

INDEX OF PLACES